PATTERN
&MOSAIC
IN THE GARDEN

PATTERN & MOSAIC
IN THE GARDEN

Clare Matthews

hamlyn

First published in Great Britain in 2003 by
Hamlyn, a division of Octopus Publishing Group Ltd
2–4 Heron Quays, London E14 4JP

ISBN 0 600 60515 9

A CIP catalogue record for this book is available
from the British Library

Printed and bound in China

10 9 8 7 6 5 4 3 2 1

Note: The author and publishers have
made every effort to ensure that all
instructions and ideas given in this book
are accurate and safe, but they cannot
accept liability for any resulting injury,
damage or loss to either person or
property whether direct or consequential
and howsoever arising.

All projects that involve electricity in the
garden, especially in relation to water
features, should be installed by a qualified
electrician and be protected by a residual
current device (circuit breaker).

For Harriet, Nancy and Joshua.

Contents

Introduction

Mosaic can bring life and interest to all parts of a garden, enriching an outside space with pattern, colour and texture that last all year round. Almost any surface can be transformed to create a decorative, eye-catching feature: walls, patios, containers, water features and furniture can be embellished to make something really individual.

With imagination, mosaic can become the perfect solution to many garden problem areas, brightening dark corners, adding colour to uninspiring walls, creating focal points or giving a new lease of life to a patio. Patterns and designs can be incredibly diverse, reflecting or creating any style or mood you choose – perhaps evoking the warmth and blue skies of the Mediterranean or the more restrained ambience of classic formality – the possibilities are endless. Mosaic also offers a chance to create something unique to reflect your own personal taste or style. However idiosyncratic, it will be your own outdoor work of art.

This book encompasses mosaic in the widest possible sense to include any pattern made up of an arrangement of smaller pieces of any material, on any surface. The techniques and skills required are straightforward and easily learned, making mosaic a valuable technique for garden owners of all abilities. Very few specialized tools or pieces of equipment are required, so the initial outlay is minimal. In addition, a whole host of inexpensive, everyday materials can be used to stunning effect – all you really need is a little imagination.

Perhaps one of the most appealing aspects of decorating the garden with pattern and mosaic is the process of creation. Working with colourful and

Above: **The simplest of materials, pebbles and slate, used imaginatively can create beautiful, durable outdoor surfaces.**

Left: **A handful of broken china has transformed a simple wall pot into something eyecatching.**

reflective materials and building up a design piece by piece is absorbing and therapeutic, while the pleasure and satisfaction in completing a piece are immense. Mosaic is a perfect outlet for creativity with plenty of scope for experimentation and invention.

Here you will find everything you need to know about creating pattern and mosaic outdoors, starting with a section of inspiration and advice on design, illustrated by brilliant mosaics in gardens all over the world. There is a basics section, describing the techniques, tools, preparation and groundwork for larger projects, including plenty of useful tips. This is followed by a range of stylish projects, with all the information you need to create them at home. The projects are designed to be copied, but once you gain confidence and master the basics they will serve as a starting point for your own exploration of the possibilities of mosaic and the thrill of decorating your garden.

Right: **The carefully chosen colour palette of this pretty stylized flower mosaic really livens up what could have been a bland rendered wall.**

Below: **Immediately familiar, reproducing a classical mosaic style creates an air of grandeur and formality.**

Below, right: **A glittering mosaic of broken mirror glass creates a fantastically reflective surface.**

INSPIRATION

Gallery of mosaic styles

The delightful examples of mosaic and pattern gathered here serve to demonstrate how diverse the art can be. Each one uses pattern and embellishment to a different end, and a large range of materials and techniques is employed. Not all are executed with great sophistication, yet the visual impact and appeal are truly inspirational.

Right: **This Australian garden is dominated by brightly coloured mosaic made from broken ceramics. The design is complemented by bold architectural plants that can hold their ground against the backdrop of such a vibrant, busy design. Waves of colour and repeated circular motifs are used to give the design coherence.**

Right: **Beautifully rounded tactile pebbles have been used to create this elegantly simple design. The small circular pebble mosaic sets off the rustic throne and together they form a calm oasis among the plants. A strong, simple motif works well in a small area of paving.**

Above: **Lapping up a rendered wall from an expanse of water, these mosaic waves are convincingly produced using remarkably few ceramic pieces. When trying to reproduce natural forms, simplifying and reducing them to a stylized form makes the task easier. The wave motif is, of course, the perfect choice to adorn a water feature while the colour of the ceramics is sympathetic to the watery theme.**

Left: **The inspiration for this intricate and extravagant mosaic was a beautifully patterned carpet. The opulent, geometric design is carefully structured by a series of boldly defined panels. The feeling is one of luxury, wealth and the exotic.**

Above: **Nestling amidst lush foliage, this mirror framed by shells, pebbles and tiles creates the illusion of a garden beyond. The materials chosen are mostly natural and in muted tones, so the mirror sits easily with the foliage. The mirror not only has the effect of suggesting a doorway, but also bounces light back into the garden, brightening a dark corner.**

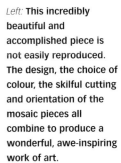

Left: **This incredibly beautiful and accomplished piece is not easily reproduced. The design, the choice of colour, the skilful cutting and orientation of the mosaic pieces all combine to produce a wonderful, awe-inspiring work of art.**

Below: **Not the most comfortable of garden seats, but perhaps one of the most striking. Large shards of mirror cover a surface punctuated with spirals of marbles. The spaces between the mosaic pieces are large and there is little attempt to contrive an exact fit. The result is an idiosyncratic piece, as much a sculpture as a seat, with tremendous appeal.**

Left: **Carefully shaped mosaic pieces reminiscent of feathers have been used to create this cockerel, used as a focal point on a brick wall. The skill and artistry employed in producing this design are considerable. The use of colour and direction in the way the pieces have been laid produces a convincingly feathery finish to this witty example of mosaic.**

Getting ideas

The inspiration for a mosaic design can come from almost anywhere. There is a rich and varied tradition to draw upon, as the art of mosaic has been used in many forms over thousands of years to enliven buildings, gardens, public spaces and interiors with pattern and colour. From the Romans who used small stone tesserae to create intricate patterns in murals and pavements, through to the rich saturated colours of Moroccan zelige work, and on to the large-scale, unrestrained mosaic style of Antonio Gaudí found in Parc Güell in Barcelona, there is a vast reservoir of colour, pattern and styles to dip into when designing a garden project.

CHOOSING A DESIGN

Practical considerations must play their part in the design process. Consider the following questions:

- what is the purpose of the mosaic or what you are trying to achieve?
- what style will best complement the garden?
- which colours are most appropriate to the design?
- what quality of materials is best suited to the project?
- at what distance will the design will be viewed?
- how much time is available to complete the project?
- what is the budget available?

Reproducing a particular style of mosaic or using certain materials can immediately conjure up a specific set of associations or ambience. For example, mimic the richly coloured geometry of the Moorish mosaic tradition to evoke the heat and spice of Marrakech or the spectacular Spanish palaces. Alternatively, encrust an object with dainty shells to conjure up a seaside holiday. Using shells on a more lavish scale has associations with shell grottoes, much in vogue with the genteel ladies of the eighteenth century who collected seashells and created their own elaborate grottoes to display them, like the one at Leeds Castle in England. So choosing the right style of decoration to suit your garden and the mood you are hoping to create is important. A container lavishly covered with sparkling azure glass tiles might be perfect in a Mediterranean-style garden but would strike a note of discord in a natural garden, where natural stone and muted tones might be more appropriate.

The mosaics of others are not the only sources of inspiration. Pattern is all around. There are flowing organic shapes like the spirals of an uncurling fern frond, the more regimented tessellations of a beehive, the manmade pattern of a fabric design and even certain types of packaging – all might provide the starting point for a design. It is rewarding to take a familiar pattern and work it in an unfamiliar medium, creating a visual or textural surprise. For example, you could use a tartan or paisley pattern on a container, such as the Pretty beaded pots on page 40.

The materials you find to hand can also help to formulate a design. Stumbling across a pile of leftover tiles, or even the accidental smashing of a cherished plate, might be the prompt to start a mosaic project. The design can evolve from what is available to create it, avoiding the sometimes arduous task of seeking the perfect materials to complete a design that you have already planned in detail.

If you are planning a large project, invest time in collecting pictures from magazines and design books, take photographs of patterns that appeal wherever you come across them and gather samples of materials that might be suitable for the project. This should produce plenty to fire your imagination when it comes to settling on the final design. Consider the materials early in the design process to ensure that your plans are realistic and achievable. If you base your ideas around a particular size or colour of pebble, you may be unable to get what you need or find it is prohibitively expensive.

Perhaps, most importantly, don't be afraid to experiment with patterns, shapes, textures and materials to produce a design that reflects your own personal style.

Left: **This mosaic water feature with intricate geometric designs is the perfect cooling centrepiece for an exotic roof terrace.**

Texture, pattern and colour

Texture, pattern and colour are the three elements that fuse to create a successful mosaic design. The three aspects are distinct but it is almost impossible to discuss one without reference to the others. Pattern is defined by using changes in colour and texture, or even either one of them. The impact of a pattern can change considerably according to the colours and textures chosen to execute it. Imagine how different a basic chequerboard design can be: worked in shining blue and yellow glass tiles it is bright and cheery, worked in matt black and white stone tiles it is formal, and worked in reclaimed brick and natural pebbles its appearance is rustic.

Some patterns and motifs are instantly recognizable and have strong associations – for example, the Greek key motif used extensively in ancient and modern Greek design, or the fleur-de-lis popular in heraldic designs. Including such patterns in a design makes an easily read statement about the style you are trying to achieve.

Choosing a pattern in proportion to the size of the project is important. Using a large repeating pattern on a small object is pointless as there is not enough space to establish the rhythm of the design. Similarly, using an intricate pattern on a large-scale pebble mosaic might look over-fussy; a bold repeated pattern is more likely to fit the bill. If a pattern has areas of great complexity, then this needs to be balanced with simplicity and calm, for example by working the design in rhythmic panels with simple borders or including restful blocks of a single colour. Repeating elements gives a pattern unity, rhythm and predictability, and this idea has been used by mosaic artists all over the world for centuries. A chaotic design has nowhere for the eye to rest and can be unsettling and unappealing.

Texture

Exciting textural contrasts can give a design added appeal – the juxtaposition of rough and smooth will highlight the textural qualities of both. Successful contrasts in texture are usually the product of the materials used. A floor of granular gravel becomes more appealing when punctuated with smooth, dense slabs of stone or sheets of Perspex. Similarly, iridescent mosaic tiles provide a powerful accent when placed in a pattern worked in natural pebbles.

Arranging pieces of the same material in a different pattern is enough to introduce subtle texture to a design. The visual texture of a surface decorated with glass mosaic tiles in a grid pattern is very different to a surface of undulating waves of similar mosaic tiles.

Above: **The pattern decorating these stone-topped walls has just enough irregularity in its design to make it lively, but enough regularity to make it cohesive. Mosaic pieces of different sizes, but of a similar shape, have been laid in a more or less consistent linear pattern to achieve this effect.**

Below: **Worked in a creeping mint, succulents and gravel, this chequerboard design is a feast of textural contrasts.**

PATTERN AND DIRECTION

Some patterns suggest movement, especially when used on a patio or path.

• If the lines of a pattern run away from you, they draw the eye (and the feet) in the same direction.

• To create a path with a more leisurely pace, plan the pattern to run across it.

• Patio surfaces are best decorated with static shapes such as circles, squares and spirals. These are restful patterns that do not suggest any movement.

COLOUR

The opportunity to add year-round colour to the garden is a thrilling prospect, but choose colours carefully to fit in with existing schemes.

• Use light, bright colours to give the garden a lift, even on sombre days.

• Use a more muted pallet to draw less attention and provide a more natural feel.

• Combine colours within a design for significant impact in the finished piece.

• Look carefully at your materials in the spot you intend to use them – often the colours will be very different *in situ*.

Below: **This formal centrepiece has been greatly enhanced by the addition of a pattern of intersecting curves of ceramic tiles. The pattern adds interest to what might otherwise be rather bland.**

Above: **The contrasting textures of rounded pebbles combined with the linear slate mulch set on edge contribute a great deal to the appeal of this organic, swirling pattern.**

Below: **This tiny, functional path encourages you to hurry along between the rows of vegetables. The bricks are laid in a herringbone pattern, with the lines running lengthways along the path, and this urges the eye and the feet along quickly.**

Above: **A muted palette and a subtle use of texture produce this tranquil, contemporary design. A frame of granite sets gives importance to the tree and a strong link to the design.**

Below: **Set between white-washed walls, these steps conjure up blue skies and warmth. Hand-painted tiles add a splash of colour to the face of the steps, which is balanced by the simplicity of practical grey pebbles on the treads.**

Materials

A myriad of everyday materials can be used to create outdoor mosaic, along with the traditional glass and stone tiles. In fact, anything that will withstand the elements can be worked into a design. Using unusual materials can increase the charm of a mosaic or contribute an element of surprise and wit.

Mosaic offers a great opportunity to recycle materials like broken china and glass or bits and pieces left over from DIY projects. The use of these types of materials is inexpensive and produces a very individual pattern. Working *objets trouvés* into a design makes a very personal, nostalgic piece. Junk shops, salvage yards, craft shops, DIY stores and sheds are treasure troves of potential mosaic materials; it's just a question of spotting them.

There are of course practical considerations in selecting materials; however seductive its appearance, a material has to match the purpose of the design. For example, when applying mosaic to a garden table, the materials have to be durable, form a flat surface and be stain resistant. If the mosaic is forming part of a patio, the materials must be frostproof and strong enough to withstand plenty of wear and tear. In wall and container decorating, there is much more freedom to experiment with any materials that catch your eye.

Glass

Glass gives a smooth, reflective quality to a mosaic. The small tesserae often used in mosaic are made from a vitreous glass. They come in a fantastic array of colours and are perfect for use outside. Glass 'gemme' tiles, shot with sparkling metals are fantastically opulent. Ordinary glass and mirror can be used for similar effects. They can either be smashed (see pages 26–7) or cut with a glasscutter. Granules of glass mulch, made from recycled bottles, can be used loose in patio surfaces or to encrust objects by pushing them into tile cement. Glass marbles and florist's beads can also be used.

Stone, pebbles and gravel

Natural stone comes in a staggering array of colours and shapes. Rounded, tactile pebbles are perfect for pebble mosaics; larger cobbles are useful for punctuating gravel surfaces, while gravel itself is incredibly versatile. Most stone is tough and durable, but soft, grainy stone will not wear well underfoot and some types of stone formed in layers are likely to flake in extreme weather. Paving slabs are a hardwearing solution for paths and patios. It is worth checking the colour of stone when it is wet as it can change dramatically. Some change from a warm tone to something drab and uninspiring.

Left: **Random pockets of sparkling green glass mulch have been used to break up the sleek surface of this geometric decking design.**

Above: **Restrained by wooden frames, organic mulches have been used to dramatic effect in this garden based on an African tribal theme.**

Right: **Ceramics, stone and mirrors combine here to produce something really special.**

Broken ceramics

Ceramic tiles and broken household china come in a wonderful range of colours and are the perfect choice to bring a splash of colour to the garden. Using broken shards also has the advantage of avoiding fiddly cutting, although ceramics can be cut if necessary. Delicate ceramics may be damaged by frost, so choose carefully.

Shells

Available from craft stores and fishmongers, shells are excellent for decorating walls and containers, conjuring up a maritime theme.

Metal

Any metal object that will not rust can be used in mosaic. Screws, spanners, nuts and bolts are all possibilities, although they are probably better suited to purely decorative work than they are to practical surfaces.

Wood

Treated wood or reclaimed railway sleepers can be used to provide a warm contrast to more severe materials. Interesting effects can be produced in paving by using small blocks of wood and displaying the end grain.

Bricks

Great for adding pattern to paved or gravelled surfaces, bricks come in a wide range of colours and finishes. Some can have a rather harsh appearance, whereas reclaimed brick gives an appealing aged and weathered finish immediately.

Above: **Cast concrete ammonites are durable and robust enough to walk on. They make an unusual addition to garden paving.**

Right: **Stepping stones of imposing slabs of slate interrupt this gravel surface – the harshness of both materials is softened by low planting.**

THE BASICS

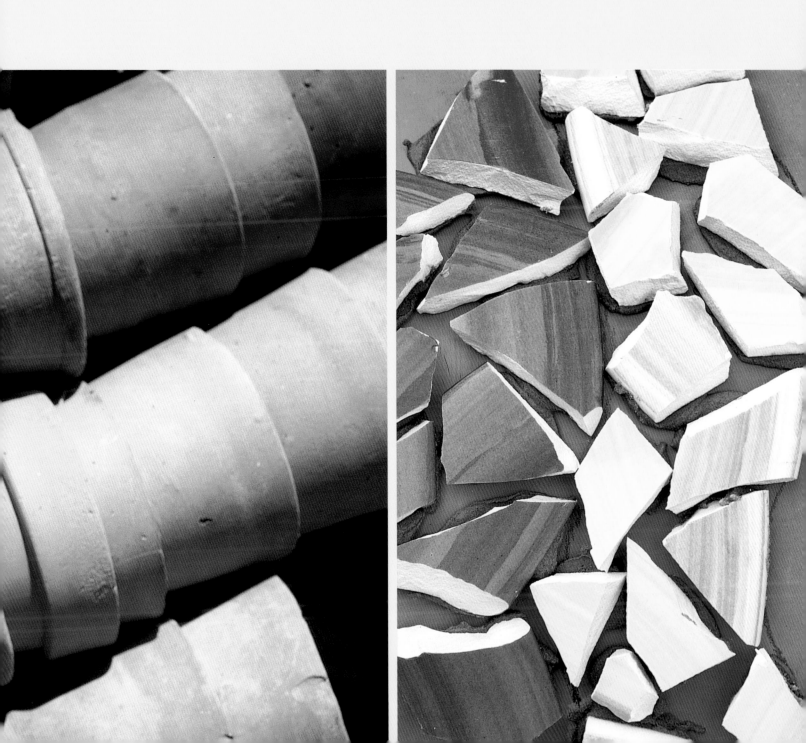

Getting started

Mosaic adds enduring pattern, life and a burst of colour to garden surfaces. The principles and techniques used to create these effects are simple to master but the results can be stunning, transforming the fabric of the garden with works that are not only beautiful but also immensely durable and practical.

The permanence and longevity of mosaic depends on following a few basic rules on the choice of materials, adhesives and preparation. Using good techniques, selecting the most appropriate materials and, for larger projects, establishing the right groundwork ensures that the finished work has the best chance of surviving the ravages of rain, sun, damp, frost and wear and tear. Preparation and groundwork are never glamorous or exciting – there is always the temptation to skimp on this part of a project and progress quickly to the more appealing task of applying shining glass tiles or arranging smooth tactile pebbles. However, apply those tiles to an ill-prepared surface or arrange those pebbles on an inadequate foundation and very soon the tiles will fall away from their base and cracks will appear in the pebble mosaic surface. It is well worth putting effort into the unseen, yet all important, preparation.

This chapter explains the basics of mosaic, everything you need to know about tools, techniques, adhesives, preparation and groundwork, so that you can confidently go on to create successful, long-lasting outdoor mosaics for your garden. It goes right back to basics with detailed step by step instructions on everything from mixing mortar to cutting tiles.

Far left: **A mixture of terracotta and blue tiles has been used to decorate these steps and wall to produce a Meditarranean feel.**

Left: **Five very different natural stones have been combined here to produce a surface that is rather 'busy'.**

Above: **Bright and cheery, ceramic tiles make an immensely durable, hardwearing decorative mosaic surface that is easily cleaned.**

Above: **The rugged sleepers that produce the pattern in this pebble path are a hardwearing structural element of the design.**

TWO TECHNIQUES

There are two main routes to bringing pattern to the garden.

• The first is surface decoration, embellishing the surface of existing features – for example brightening up a weathered old table, cladding a shady wall with colour or perhaps creating a show-stopping, colourful container from a bland terracotta pot.

• The second is where the decorative materials form an integral part of the structure, a technique common to paths and terraces – the design is literally built into the structure.

THE PRINCIPLES

Whatever the materials being used to adorn the surface of an object and whatever that object might be, the fundamentals of the process are the same. The pieces of material are stuck to the object with tile adhesive and then the spaces between the pieces of decorative material are filled with grout to form a continuous resilient surface. The technique can be used in different ways: if you select the best method coupled with the correct adhesive and grout for the task, almost anything can be decorated and all sorts of materials can be used to create mosaic.

Surface decoration

There are two ways of applying surface decoration. First is the direct method, where the pattern is drawn onto the object and the mosaic pieces are applied one by one to build up the pattern. The second is the indirect method where the pattern is drawn onto brown paper and the decorative materials temporarily glued to the paper in the correct pattern. The whole design is then applied to the object in one piece. Direct mosaic laying is useful for uneven, irregular surfaces and when a combination of different or uneven materials is being used. The indirect method is useful on flat surfaces, like tables, where a level finish is required; this allows a design to be perfected before it is pushed into place.

SURFACE PREPARATION

The surface to be decorated needs careful preparation.

- All surfaces need to be clean, dry and sound.
- Porous surfaces like terracotta and wood must be sealed with diluted PVA before the decoration is applied.
- Any wood used to support mosaics must be suitable for external use to prevent rotting.

Direct technique

1 Use a pencil to draw the design directly onto the object to be decorated with mosaic. Any mistakes and corrections will be covered with mosaic. Intricate designs can be laid out on a piece of paper first. Draw the design on a piece of paper. The mosaic pieces can be cut if necessary and laid out on the paper and then the pattern can be transferred to the object piece by piece.

2 If the object is porous, terracotta for example, seal the surface with PVA diluted 1:1 with water. Apply the PVA with a brush and leave it to dry before decorating.

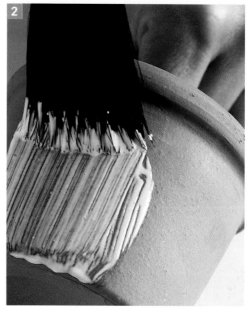

3 Now start the mosaic pattern. Apply the pieces of mosaic, either by spreading a small area with adhesive and pushing in the mosaic pieces or by applying the adhesive to the back of each piece, a technique known as 'buttering'. Wear gloves to protect your hands from contact with the tile adhesive and grout.

4 After buttering the backs of the tiles, press them into place on the object, using the pencil marks as a guide.

5 Allow the adhesive to dry overnight. Then use a sharp tool to remove any excess adhesive that might stick up above the surface of the tiles after grouting.

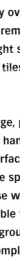

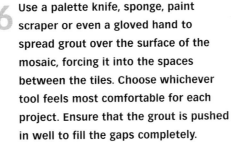

6 Use a palette knife, sponge, paint scraper or even a gloved hand to spread grout over the surface of the mosaic, forcing it into the spaces between the tiles. Choose whichever tool feels most comfortable for each project. Ensure that the grout is pushed in well to fill the gaps completely.

7 Use a damp sponge or cloth to wipe away the excess grout from the surface of the mosaic. Rinse the sponge or cloth frequently and wipe the work several times until there are neat seams of grout flush with the surface of the tiles.

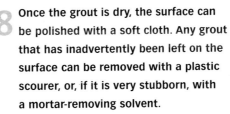

8 Once the grout is dry, the surface can be polished with a soft cloth. Any grout that has inadvertently been left on the surface can be removed with a plastic scourer, or, if it is very stubborn, with a mortar-removing solvent.

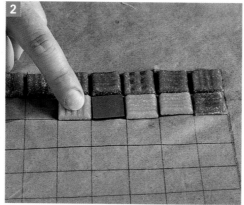

Indirect technique

1 Accurately measure the surface to be decorated and draw the shape onto the matt side of a piece of brown parcel paper, using a pencil. Next, draw on the design, remembering to reverse it if it is not symmetrical. If necessary, the pattern can be coloured to make it easier to follow, providing the materials being used are not porous and will not be stained by the colours.

2 Using water-soluble gum or dilute water-soluble PVA glue, attach the mosaic tiles or decoration to the paper, face down, gradually building up the design. There is plenty of time to perfect the pattern. When all the pieces are stuck in place, trim the paper flush with the design.

3 At this stage it is possible to grout the design to prevent adhesive pushing through onto the face of the tiles. To do this, use a sponge or gloved hand to spread grout over the back of the tiles, working it uniformly into the spaces between them. Use a damp cloth or sponge to remove all the excess grout. This step is optional.

4 Spread adhesive evenly on the surface being decorated, here a plain tile, using a notched trowel or comb to create a grooved surface. Do not use the comb too heavily or areas of adhesive may be removed completely. This grooved bed of adhesive will provide a better key or grip the design more efficiently than a flat bed of adhesive. Now work quickly to apply the mosaic.

5 Carefully line up one edge of the mosaic on the surface and lower it into position. Applying pressure as evenly as possible, press the mosaic into the bed of adhesive. Leave it to dry.

6 Thoroughly moisten the brown paper using a wet sponge and wait a few minutes for the glue to dissolve. Starting at one corner, slowly peel the paper away from the tiles. If any pieces of mosaic come away with the paper, simply remove them and glue them back into the design.

7 Now follow the instructions for grouting from step 6 onwards of the Direct Technique (see pages 22–3). Even if you chose to grout the design before it was applied it will require re-grouting.

Tools, equipment and safety

Applying mosaic does not require a great investment in specialized tools; many of the tools required are used for everyday tiling jobs, while others are likely to be in the home already. The tools needed will vary according to the project.

Tools for cutting

Tile nippers Used to cut and shape glass, porcelain and ceramic mosaic materials. They have two cutting edges that come together, cutting the material between them as the handles are squeezed tight. To cut brittle materials, position the blades at the edge of the piece to prevent shattering.

Tile cutters Used to cut tiles by first scoring the tile with a cutting wheel and then snapping it by pinching it along the scored line with the snapper. This tool is excellent for cutting large ceramic tiles. A metal rule is used to ensure that the scored line is accurate.

Small hammer Used for smashing tiles, crockery and glass into random-shaped pieces. The hammer does not need to be heavy as the materials used are easily broken.

Tools for application

Plastic combs and 'squeegees' Used for applying grout, these come in various shapes and sizes. Small areas can be grouted using a small plastic comb. For larger areas, a rubber-edged squeegee may be useful. For very large areas, use a flatbed squeegee.

Palette knives and modelling tools There are many small tools available in this category. Some have blunt square ends, others are pointed, and many have two different ends. It is well worth having one in your tool kit for applying adhesive to curved and uneven surfaces.

Paint scraper Used to apply grout and adhesive.

Notched float or comb Used to spread a grooved bed of adhesive and provide a better key for the mosaic pieces. Often, tile adhesives come with one.

Cloths and sponges Used damp to remove excess grout, and dry to polish the finished piece.

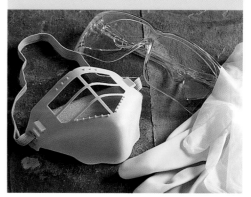

Tips and techniques

These few simple tips and techniques will allow you to tackle any of the projects in this book with confidence.

Smashing ceramics and glass

A gentle tap with a hammer is all that is required to produce randomly shaped pieces of varying sizes from a ceramic tile, crockery, glass or mirror. The process is hard to control and can produce flying shards that are razor sharp, so wear protective gloves, safety goggles and place a tea towel or thick cloth over the material while it is being smashed.

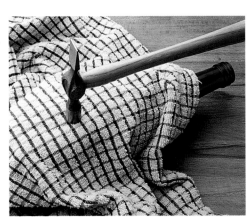

Cutting tiles

Use a special tile cutter; with practice this tool allows you to make identically shaped pieces again and again.

1 First score the tile using the cutting wheel, applying firm even pressure and using a metal rule as a guide.

2 Next grip the tile with the scored line in the middle of the snapper and squeeze while supporting the tile with your other hand.

3 The tile should break cleanly into two pieces along the scored line.

Making small shapes

Mosaic materials such as ceramics, glass and porcelain can be cut and nibbled into smaller shapes using tile nippers.

1 Small mosaic tiles can be cut accurately in half and then, if required, into quarters to produce either squares or triangles.

2 The blades of the nippers should be positioned at the edge of the piece to avoid shattering.

3 Other shapes, such as circles, can be cut by repeatedly nibbling away at the edges of a piece to achieve the perfect shape. Work around the edges of a fragment of ceramic or a glass mosaic tile, removing small pieces until you have the desired shape.

4 To make small squares out of a larger tile, cut the tile into strips using a tile cutter. Then use the tile nippers to cut the strip into small even squares.

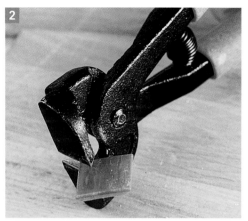

Adhesives and grout for outdoor mosaics

Outdoor mosaic projects must be weatherproof, so use a tile adhesive and grout made specifically for use outside. These are cement based and usually come in powder form; the powder is mixed with water to produce a workable consistency. There are many different brands available, so it is wise to check the manufacturer's information for advice on the proportion of water required in mixing and to assess the suitability of a product for a particular project.

Cement-based adhesive and grout is suitable for use on most surfaces and materials, using the direct and indirect method. Specialized, highly flexible adhesives are necessary when working on metal or plastic surfaces, as these surfaces expand and contract with temperature change.

COLOURED GROUT

Grout is available in white or grey, but it can also be coloured.

- Grey or white grout creates a neutral background emphasizing the mosaic material.
- A coloured grout can have a dramatic impact on the finished mosaic.
- Grouts are generally coloured by mixing special powdered pigments with the grout powder before the water is added.
- Another method is to add acrylic paints to the grout mixture; this produces great colours and is worth experimenting with.
- A consistent grout colour is important to the finished effect, so when mixing coloured grout

be accurate in your measuring, or mix up sufficient grout to complete the job in one batch in order to maintain a constant colour.

GROUT SEALANTS

For tabletops and other vulnerable surfaces, it is worth applying a proprietary grout sealant to protect them from staining.

Marking out

Once you have decided on the location and dimensions of a project, it is necessary to mark its exact boundaries with sand, string or spray paint so you know where to start digging. For patio and path projects the first step is marking out.

Paths

1 For straight paths mark out one side of the path following step 1 of Rectangles and squares (see opposite, below left).

2 Locate the other side by measuring off this string line at right angles at regular intervals along its length and mark it out.

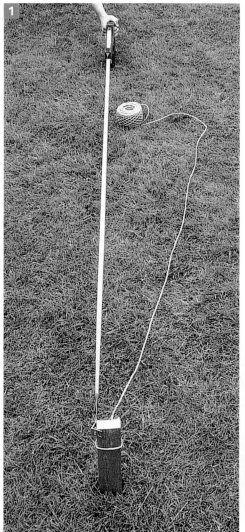

Marking out circles

1 Push a peg into the centre of the area where your circle is to be positioned and tie a string loosely to it so that it can move freely round the peg as you walk around it.

2 Measure the desired radius of the circle along the length of the string and, using a trail of sand or a can of spray paint, mark the circumference of the circle by pulling the string taut and moving around the peg. Continue moving around the peg until the circle is complete.

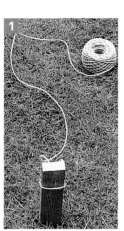

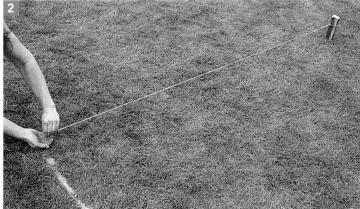

Rectangles and squares

1 Drive in a wooden marker peg at one corner of your rectangle or square and use a tape measure to calculate where the next peg should go. Drive in another peg at the second corner. Tie a string between the two pegs.

2 Locate the third corner by pulling the string off the second post at a right angle and measuring along it the correct distance with the tape measure. Drive in a peg to mark the exact position of the third corner, attach the string and repeat to mark the final corner. The string can be replaced with sand or spray paint.

Groundwork

Good design and durable materials are not the only factors in successfully incorporating pattern into the garden – good preparation and the quality of the groundwork are equally important. Sound groundwork is crucial if a surface is to withstand the punishment of the elements and stand up to the trials of wear and tear without crumbling.

The principles are straightforward and simple to implement. The aim is to construct a firm base that will not move, to which the decorative surface can be securely attached. In essence, this involves removing the topsoil to a level where the ground is stable and filling the void with a layer of compacted hardcore and perhaps concrete, on which the surface design can be built.

Excavation

All vegetation must be removed and the topsoil dug out from the marked-out area. The exact depth you dig will depend on the surface material being used and the soil type. The softer or wetter the ground, the more soil has to be removed and the deeper the layer of hardcore must be to create a stable base. If you have any doubts, it is always best to seek the advice of a professional.

Usually a depth of 10–15cm (4–6in), plus the depth of the mortar bed, is sufficient and the surface material. Try to dig out the area evenly and check the depth as work progresses. The final excavation cannot be completed until the levels have been established (see opposite).

The base

The excavated area is first filled with a layer of hardcore. This usually takes the form of crushed stone in a range of sizes, from large pieces to dust. The large and small pieces can be compacted together to form a firm, level layer, the smaller pieces filling the gaps between the larger. This type of material is unlikely either to deteriorate or to absorb water. Builder's rubble is sometimes used as hardcore, although it can be uneven and harder to work with.

Smaller areas of hardcore can be compacted with a hand rammer or even using a heavy garden roller. For larger areas it is advisable to hire a machine known as a whacker plate. The finished compacted layer of hardcore should be at least 10–15cm (4–6in) deep.

Left: **During excavation the vegetation and topsoil are removed and levelled to allow the construction of a firm base.**

Middle: **Compacted hardcore is used to create a stable base. It is normally supplied as crushed stone, but builder's rubble could be used instead.**

Right: **Once they are fully compacted the pieces of hardcore pack tightly together to provide a sound level base for the paving.**

Working out the fall

In laying a solid paved surface you are creating an area that water cannot drain through, so it is important that flat paved surfaces have a fall or slight slope built into them to ensure rainwater can drain away efficiently and does not form puddles on the surface. The more uneven the surface materials the greater the fall or slope must be. It is most important that the slope should be such that the water drains away from houses, walls or other buildings to an area where it can drain away freely. The uneven, knobbly surface of a pebble mosaic would need a fall of about 25mm over 1 metre, that is to say a pebble mosaic patio 4 metres wide would be about 10 centimetres lower at one end than the other. More even materials need a fall of 25mm over 1.5 metres to allow rainwater to drain effectively.

Put in a peg a little higher than the final surface level. This will be the point of reference against which all levels are measured known as a datum.

Measure down from the top of the datum peg to the desired surface level at the highest point of the project. Use a spirit level to ensure accuracy. The highest point should be the point nearest the house or any other structure. Put in a peg so that its top marks this level.

Add this figure to the fall required over the length of the paved surface (see above). Extend a string line from the top of the datum peg to the lower end of the project and holding the string taut and, using a spirit level to ensure the string is level, measure the distance calculated down from the stringline. Put in a peg with its top at this level. This shows the finished level of the paving at the lowest point.

A string between the level marker peg at the top of the project and that at the bottom would lie along the surface of the finished project. These markers should be referred to as the surface is laid to achieve the correct fall. Large projects may require several level markers arranged at intervals across the project so that the levels can easily be checked.

Above: **Always use a spirit level to ensure your patio will be an even surface.**

Left: **A fall of 25mm over 1500mm will be sufficient to clear water from this flat brick surface.**

Right: **A substantial project such as this impressive flight of steps will require considerable groundwork and foundations and are best left to the professionals or experienced amateur.**

Mortar and concrete

Mortar is made by mixing cement with sand and water and is used to lay bricks and paving and to make pebble mosaics. Sometimes a plasticizer is added to make the mortar easier to work with, although a good squirt of washing-up liquid in the mix has the same effect. Concrete is made by mixing cement with ballast or aggregate and water, and is used to construct foundations and paths. Mortar is a smooth mixture, whereas concrete is much coarser because it contains stones and other chunky material.

Both mortar and concrete can be purchased ready mixed in bags, just requiring the addition of water. This makes life simple for small projects but would be prohibitively expensive for larger ones. It is also possible to buy concrete ready mixed, but this is only feasible where large quantities are required and when you can use it within a few hours of delivery.

The proportions of sand or ballast to cement will dictate the strength of the finished mortar or concrete. Different mixes are suited to different jobs. The mix is always expressed as a ratio of cement to sand. 1:6 is a good all-round mortar mix suitable for most projects, whereas 1:4, a slightly stronger mix, is needed if you are using a dry mix.

Once you know the correct proportions for the project, it is a simple matter of measuring the cement, sand or ballast by the shovel- or bucketful. For example, a 1:6 mortar mix requires one shovel of cement to six of sand.

The exact amount of water required is a matter of judgement. Adding a little water at a time is the best approach, and, if the mix becomes too sloppy, it is perfectly acceptable to add a little more of each of the dry ingredients to firm it up. The final mix should be soft and pliable, neither too crumbly nor too sloppy. The more water you add, the weaker the final result will be.

Concrete and mortar become solid through a chemical reaction between the cement and water – after about ten hours the mixture solidifies but it continues to harden and strengthen for up to seven days so always allow strengthening time.

Left: **A dry mix of sand and cement can be used where a wet mortar mix would be difficult to use. A dry mix (of sand and cement) has been brushed between the slim fragments of this slate surface; once dampened the dry mix solidifies holding the fragments firmly in place.**

TIPS FOR WORKING WITH CEMENT

- Store cement and ready-mixed products under cover and off the ground. If they absorb any moisture they will harden in the bag.
- Don't use cement products in freezing weather conditions. This produces a weak mix in which cracks will form later on.
- Add interest to a project by adding a powdered colorant to the mixture. These are available from builder's merchants.
- Cement can cause skin irritation and dryness so it is advisable to wear gloves whenever you are working with it.

Mixing mortar and concrete

Small amounts of mortar or concrete can be mixed on a wooden or plastic board, in a wheelbarrow or even in a bucket. Where larger quantities are required, a cement mixer makes the task easier. The measured sand and cement are added to the drum and mixed together, then the water is added while the drum is turning.

1 Measure out the sand using a shovel and put it on a large board or plastic sheet. Place the correct quantity of cement to achieve the mix you require on top.

2 Mix the sand and cement evenly by turning them over with the shovel, continuing until the colour of the mix is consistent.

3 Form the mixture into a mound and make a well in the centre. Add a small amount of water to the well.

4 Turn in the sides of the crater and keep turning the mixture with the shovel to incorporate the water. If more water is required make a well and add more water, mixing as before.

5 Turn the mixture over and use chopping movements with the spade held vertically until the mix is an even colour and consistency.

USING A DRY MIX

A dry mix is a blend of sand and cement which is used as a bed for some paving materials. It can also be brushed into the spaces between paving materials, such as the pebbles in a pebble mosaic. Water is added later to moisten the mixture and set the mortar.

DECORATIVE
CONTAINERS

Adding mosaic to containers is a quick and easy way to bring a splash of colour to the garden. Whether they are arranged in groups on terraces, in a row on a windowsill or used as an attention-grabbing focal point, decorated containers are perfect for enhancing the garden's structure. Lavishly planted, a container can take centre stage for a season, and, once the blooms fade, it can be replanted for a whole new look next season. When enlivened with mosaic, the most humble of containers can become a decorative piece in its own right, with no need for planting.

When choosing a colour or design for a container, it is worth considering how it will be planted as well as the style and ambience of its chosen location. Selecting colours and textures that successfully set off the planting will increase the impact of the container; yellows and greens work well with the fresh foliage of herbs, blue containers show off yellow and orange blooms beautifully while metallic materials complement the fleshy leaves of succulents and look chic planted with cool silvers and whites.

The limited scale of container projects makes them an excellent choice for beginners to develop their skills. Containers present the opportunity to practise techniques and experiment with design, materials and colour combinations, at little expense – the perfect way to gain confidence before tackling larger projects.

Concrete, terracotta, stone, metal and even rigid plastic containers can be transformed using a whole range of surface materials. Simply shaped containers are much easier to decorate; working over the curves and fluting of an ornate pot is fiddly and can produce an untidy, confused result. Often it is easier to smooth out the fine detail on the container with a thick bed of suitable adhesive.

The container must be clean, free from loose flakes and dust and absolutely dry. Porous containers such as terracotta, concrete and stone should be coated with a PVA sealant before they are decorated. Use a flexible cement-based adhesive on metal or plastic containers that may expand or contract with temperature change. This will allow the mosaic decoration to move with the container, rather than being forced off the surface.

The mosaic surface on a container is purely decorative; it needs to stand up to the elements but other than that there are no practical demands on it. This makes containers perfect for experimenting with unusual and fragile materials, such as shells, thin ceramics, buttons, beads, wire and glass. Don't feel that it is essential to apply mosaic to the whole container; lively, eye-catching containers can be created by applying decoration to a single area of the pot, perhaps a prominent panel or rim. To save time, combine applied decoration with a lick of brightly coloured paint to produce striking results.

Above: **Worked around a re-formed central motif, the fragments of blue and white china used to decorate this standard flower pot are linked by a subtle blue grout that pulls the design together.**

Right: **A host of different bits and pieces adorn this container – its surface is encrusted with pebbles, ceramics and shells to produce a very individual piece.**

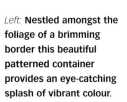

Left: **Nestled amongst the foliage of a brimming border this beautiful patterned container provides an eye-catching splash of vibrant colour.**

Mediterranean wall pots

The blues, yellows and oranges of these simple wall pots are evocative of the azure skies and warmth of the Mediterranean.

SHOPPING LIST
3 terracotta wall pots
PVA glue
4 blue, yellow and orange dinner plates
grey cement-based adhesive
grey cement-based grout

TOOLS
pencil
small hammer
paintbrush
tea towel
palette knife
sponge
dry cloth

Planted with cascading red and orange portulaca, these pots can bring life and colour to any sunny wall. The chunky, colour-washed china used to decorate the plain pots adds to their character. Using broken crockery inevitably leads to a slightly uneven finish, but this is all part of the charm. The random pieces are applied to the pot so that they fit together loosely; the more effort you put into contriving this, fit the tidier the end result will appear. Lively results, however, can be achieved with little attention.

1 Use a pencil to draw an undulating band about 4cm (1½in) from the top of each pot; any mistakes at this stage will be hidden. Next seal the terracotta pots by painting with a coat of PVA diluted in equal quantities with water.

2 Smash the crockery using a small hammer, covering it with a tea towel if the pieces are flying around. Check the size of the fragments at intervals and stop when the pieces are about 2cm (¾in) long. Producing fragments of approximately equal size will give a more uniform, neat finish.

3 Use the buttering technique (see pages 22–3) to apply pieces of china to the band. Butter each piece of china with adhesive using a palette knife and push it firmly into place on the pot. Define the edges of the band of decoration as accurately as possible.

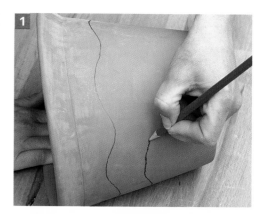

IDEAS TO INSPIRE

• A set of three blue pots would work well planted with the scarlet geraniums that characterize much of the Mediterranean, especially if you have a rendered wall to hang them on.

• A group of three pots – one blue, one yellow and one orange – would make an equally striking display, especially if they were united by identical or similar planting.

• Broken ceramic tiles would work well instead of or as well as the crockery.

4 When the band is complete, cover the rest of the pot with pieces of china of a contrasting colour, using the same technique. Ensure that none of the pieces protrudes above the pot rim. Decorate the base of the pot in the same way, or just make a neat edge on the bottom rim. Leave to dry.

5 Mix up enough grout for all three pots and use a sponge to push grout into the gaps between the pieces of china. Once the joints are evenly filled, wash the sponge and use it to remove the grout from the surface of the crockery, rinsing it regularly. Finally polish off the surface with a dry cloth.

Pretty beaded pots

This group of three pretty pots in matching saucers makes an appealing centrepiece for a garden dining table or a windowsill.

A lick of lilac paint provides the perfect foil for the sparkling bead motifs, which are produced by the indirect technique of mosaic. The seemingly delicate glass beads are durable enough to be used outside but are incredibly fiddly to work with; creating the design on brown paper allows the beads to be arranged perfectly before they are transferred to the surface of the pots. Tweezers make it easier to manipulate the beads. The vivid colour of the pots gives them appeal at a distance, while the intricate beaded design is best appreciated close up. Providing each pot with its own matching saucer looks appealing and prevents staining on surfaces.

SHOPPING LIST

3 terracotta pots, about 10cm (4in) in
    diameter
3 terracotta saucers
lilac outdoor terracotta or masonry paint
1 sheet of brown parcel paper
water-soluble gum or PVA glue
250 (approx.) glass beads, both round and
    bugle-shaped
grey cement-based adhesive

TOOLS

paintbrush
pencil
circular template
tweezers
scissors
small palette knife
damp cloth or sponge
soft dry cloth

1 Paint the pots and saucers with the paint. Ensure the pots are clean, dry and free from dust, then apply the paint with a paintbrush and allow to dry.

2 Now make the motifs; draw 24 circles onto the brown paper using a pencil and a 2cm (¾in) template.

3 Coat one of the circles with glue and carefully arrange the beads within the circle. Place a small round bead at the centre, four pairs of bugle beads to form a cross shape, a pair of contrasting, shorter bugle beads between each arm and a small round bead between each arm of the pair. Repeat this until all of the circles are complete.

4 When the glue is completely dry, cut around the motifs, taking care not to dislodge any of the beads.

5 Use a pencil to mark the positions of eight motifs on each pot, so that there is a ring of four about 2cm (¾in) from the top of the pot and another, offset, about 4cm (1½in) up from the base of the pot.

6 Take one motif and butter the bead side with adhesive (see pages 22–3). You should use enough for the beads to bed into but not enough to squash out of the sides when the motif is pushed onto the pot. This will probably be a matter of trial and error.

7 Firmly push one motif onto each of the marked positions. Apply even pressure all over the surface ensuring the whole motif is in contact with the surface of the pot. If any adhesive is squeezed out, remove it with a cloth. Repeat with all of the motifs and leave to dry.

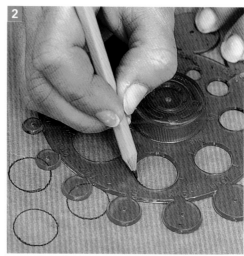

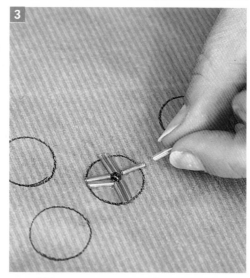

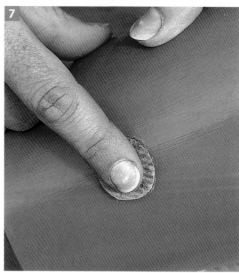

8 Working on one pot at a time, use a damp cloth or sponge, to wet the brown paper on the motifs thoroughly. Leave for a few moments for the glue to dissolve.

9 Carefully peel away the brown paper discs to reveal the beads embedded in the adhesive. Gently polish the surface with a soft cloth. It is possible that some beads may come away with the paper; simply use a small amount of adhesive to replace them.

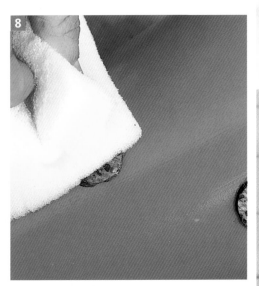

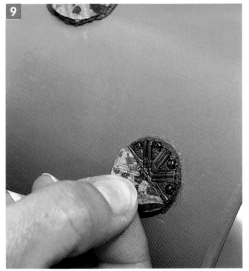

• Paint some pots with silver paint and decorate them with plain crystal beads. These would look fantastic planted with fleshy succulents, such as *Echeveria agavoides* or *Graptopetalum paraguayense* (mother-of- pearl plant), which have a greyish bloom on their leaves.

• The whole project could be scaled up – larger beads could be used to create bigger motifs to adorn larger pots.

• A quick and easy way of making use of tiny, sparkly beads is to cover a pot with a layer of adhesive and roll the pot in the beads until the whole surface is encrusted.

Daisy trough

Embellish a sturdy trough with a striking panel of mosaic decoration to transform it into a unique garden feature.

This trough will attract attention and cheer up the garden all year round. It would also make a perfect windowbox as it is attractive when viewed from all angles and would create an enticing link between the house and garden, whatever the season.

Here, only the central panel of the trough has been decorated – most troughs have this relatively flat expanse, which is easier to decorate than the curving surface of a pot. Leaving the top and bottom rims untouched has the effect of framing the mosaic, giving it emphasis, and preserves what is most attractive about the character of the trough.

The three designs featured here all use ceramic tiles, but the tiles have been cut and broken in different ways to create three very different designs.

SHOPPING LIST

For a trough 50 x 20 x 20cm
1 large terracotta trough
PVA glue
1 yellow ceramic tile
cement-based tile adhesive
3 white ceramic tiles
6–8 plum ceramic tiles
10–12 mauve ceramic tiles
white cement-based grout

TOOLS

pencil
round object for template
ruler
paintbrush
small hammer
tea towel
tile nippers
tile cutter
small palette knife
grouting squeegee
damp sponge
dry cloth

1 Use a pencil to mark the design on the trough. First draw a series of circles evenly spaced around the outside, using the base of a flowerpot or a cup as a template, if necessary. The circles should be about 10cm (4in) across and at least 2cm (¾in) apart.

2 Next mark a band 2.5cm (1in) wide at the top and bottom of the panel to be decorated. Use the template on page 122 as a guide. Seal the trough with PVA glue diluted in equal quantities with water.

3 Break a yellow tile into pieces with the hammer and tea towel. Take a small fragment and produce a roughly circular centre for one of the daisies by nibbling around its edge with nippers (see pages 26–7). Produce as many centres as you have circles on the trough.

4 Use the scoring wheel of the tile cutter to score a number of strips about 1cm (⅜in) wide on a white tile. Use a metal ruler as a guide.

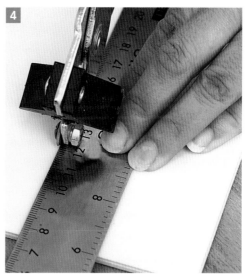

5 Use the snapping plate of the tile cutter to break the tile into strips. Then use the tile nippers to cut the strips into approximately 3cm (1¼in) lengths. Make six strips for each daisy.

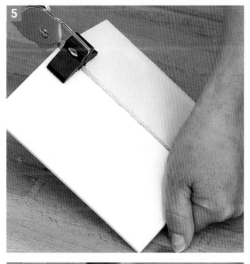

6 Butter the yellow centres with adhesive (see pages 22–3) and push each firmly into position at the centre of each daisy, that is, at the centre of each of the marked pencil circles.

7 Butter each of the white petals in turn and arrange six around each yellow centre, with their outer tips touching the pencil circles. Arrange the petals of each daisy in a similar pattern.

8 Use a small hammer to break the other tiles. Cover the tiles with a tea towel and gently tap them to produce pieces of around 2.5cm (1in).

9 Butter pieces of plum tile and fill in the borders at the top and bottom of the design. Try to arrange the pieces so that there is a loose fit – they don't need to fit together perfectly.

10 When the borders are complete, fill in the background around the daisies and up to the border with pieces of mauve tile. When the design is complete, leave the adhesive to dry.

11 Use a squeegee to apply the grout over the surface of the design, forcing it into the gaps between the fragments of tile. Take care to avoid spreading grout on the bare terracotta rims and remove any stray grout immediately.

12 Use a damp sponge to remove the excess grout from the face of the tiles, rinsing it out several times to avoid smearing. Continue until the face of the tiles is clean of grout.

13 Finally, after about 15 minutes, polish the surface of the tiles with a dry cloth to remove any smears. Leave the mosaic to dry completely before planting.

IDEAS TO INSPIRE

Below: This fresh, fragrant herb garden has been created by decorating the trough with ceramic tiles cut (11 green and 14 yellow) into more or less square shapes, imitating the uniformity of glass mosaic tesserae. The regularity of the mosaic pieces is well suited to this geometric design (see template on page 122). The process of first scoring and snapping the tiles into strips and then nipping them into squares is time-consuming, but the results make it well worth while. The clean, crisp combination of yellow and green make the perfect foil for the lush foliage of culinary herbs.

Above: Blowsy yellow tulips echo the striking blocks of yellow tile pieces set amidst the random orange fragments on this trough. This simple design (see template on page 122), using 2 yellow and 22 orange tiles relies on contrasting colour and juxtapositing regularity and irregularity for its impact. The bold scheme needs bold planting and the bright yellow tulip, 'Mr Van der Hoef', is perfect.

Simple, stylish pot rims

These dazzling containers are quick and easy to make and bring colour and fun to any corner of the garden.

Combining mosaic with paint means a basic flowerpot, however large, can be transformed quickly, using very little decorative material. The standard flowerpot shape is best suited to this treatment as its prominent rim is well defined and easy to decorate.

This really is an opportunity to have fun and be innovative. These pots require little investment of time or money so you can afford to be daring with materials – try the outrageous, even if it only lasts a season.

SHOPPING LIST

3 terracotta flowerpots of different sizes
pink, yellow and green paint suitable for
    outdoor terracotta or masonry
1 roll of lead-free soldering flux
cement-based tile adhesive
15 glass florist's beads
a selection of small shells
40 glass stars
white cement-based grout

TOOLS

paintbrush
wooden spoon
wire cutters
palette knife
damp sponge

1 Paint the clean, dry flower pots with the paints, one in each colour (in this case, pink was used for the large pot, yellow for the middle one and green for the smallest). Leave to dry.

2 Cut a length of soldering flux and wind it around the spoon handle to form a spiral. The hole left at the centre of the spiral should be large enough for a glass bead. Wrap the flux around the handle four or five times. Make enough spirals to decorate the rim of the pink pot.

3 Apply adhesive to one side of a spiral and press it onto the rim of the pot. Use the damp sponge to wipe away any adhesive that squeezes out. Repeat round the rim.

4 Butter the back of a glass bead with adhesive and push it firmly into the centre of the spiral. Repeat this until all the spirals are filled.

5 To decorate the yellow pot, spread a bed of adhesive onto the rim of the pot, about 5cm (2in) at a time, and press the shells into the adhesive, arranging them as closely together as possible. Continue right around the rim to form a continuous band. Allow to dry before planting.

6 To decorate the green pot, butter the glass stars with tile adhesive and stick them to the rim of the pot. Mix a little of the green paint with some of the white tile grout and use it to grout the spaces between the stars. Getting a perfect colour match is a matter of trial and error; mix enough white grout to finish the whole pot and add a little green paint. If the colour is too pale, add a little more until the match is perfect.

IDEAS TO INSPIRE

The tiny shells decorating the rim of the sunny yellow pot become almost indistinguishable once they are crammed together to create a continuous band of texture and colour. Shining glass stars add a touch of glitter to the lime green pot. The stars are surrounded by pale green grout which has been made by mixing a little of the green paint into the grout.

WATER

Decorative mosaic is the perfect embellishment for water features. The reflective surface of many mosaic materials associates beautifully with the sparkling surface of moving water: both gleam as sunlight plays upon them. Many mosaic materials will survive the action of water completely undamaged, with their pattern and colour shining through the water. The art of mosaic has a traditional association with water; this association no doubt springs from the durability of traditional mosaic tesserae and their ability to survive complete submersion if required.

A well-designed water feature makes a captivating point of interest in a garden – whether the dynamic, sparkling gush from a fountain, the still, reflective surface of a small pool or a haven for aquatic plants and wildlife. Incorporating water into a garden brings a plethora of possibilities. Decorative mosaic can be used to ornament many different types of water feature, and the design and the materials chosen can complement any garden surroundings.

The simplest way to create a mosaic water feature is by decorating something you've bought, customizing it perfectly to reflect your style and taste. There are a multitude of fountains, overflowing urns, waterspouts and reproduction millstones available, many of which are suitable for decoration. If you decide to take this option remember that simple shapes, like the circle of a millstone, will be easier to decorate.

The alternative is to create something from scratch. This is not as daunting as it might sound: a piece of marine plywood is an inviting blank canvas for mosaic and makes an excellent backing for a water spout. Add a wall pot containing a pump to the sheet of marine plywood and it becomes a self-contained wall fountain, ideal for bringing the sound and sparkle of moving water to even the smallest of spaces. A pond can be given a boost by an edging of concrete paving stones covered in mosaic; schemes can be devised to complement both formal and informal ponds.

The materials used to decorate water features must not only suit the design but also withstand the action of water. Glass mosaic tiles, broken bottles, glass marbles, glass mulch and some ceramics will withstand complete immersion. Other materials associate well with water, such as mirror glass and more delicate ceramics, but are best reserved for areas that receive the occasional splash. Any metal that corrodes should be completely avoided, as not only will its surface corrode but it also will potentially stain the whole mosaic. The adhesive and grout used for any water feature project should be suitable for use underwater. All water features are prone to a build-up of green algae; it can be scrubbed away, but a better solution is to stop it building up at all by using products available from aquatic suppliers.

All pumps need a permanent electricity supply installed by a qualified electrician, and must be protected by a residual current device (circuit breaker).

Opposite, above: **Here, abstract blocks of colour echo the fractured, moving surface of the water.**

Opposite, below: **Used to create two distinct patterns, brightly coloured tesserae decorate this stunning water sculpture.**

Right: **This quirky, cascading fountain employs skilfully arranged shells to create an unusual fountain head.**

Mirrored fish fountain

This self-contained water feature will bring the sparkle and calming sound of moving water to the smallest of spaces.

SHOPPING LIST

1 piece of 1.8cm (¹¹⁄₁₆in) thick marine plywood at least 80 x 60cm (32 x 24in)
PVA glue
1 terracotta wall pot
2 stainless steel nuts and bolts
blue adhesive or mortar colorizer
white cement-based, waterproof tile adhesive
200 small blue marbles
mirror glass
grey cement-based grout
1 small pond pump
1 piece clear water pipe with a 16mm diameter, approx. 50cm (20in) long
silicone sealant
20 large soap bubble marbles and glass shells

TOOLS

saw
paintbrush
pencil
drill and drill bits
spanner
paint scraper
palette knife
tea towel
small hammer
tile nippers
sponge or grouting squeegee
damp sponge

There are many different pumps available, so ask your supplier which is most suited to your needs. They will need to know how far the water has to be pumped and the diameter of the spout. Some pumps are adjustable, so you can create a pleasing flow of water. Remember always to ensure that the water in the pot is topped up to avoid the pump's motor burning out.

1 Cut the plywood into a rectangle 80 x 60cm (32 x 24in). Seal the plywood and the wall pot, inside and out, with a coat of PVA diluted with equal quantities of water.

2 Draw the fish motif onto the board using the template on page 123 as a guide. Mark the positions of the wall pot and its fixings. Also mark the positions of a hole just above the wall pot for the pipe from the pump, the spout in the fish's mouth and a hole at each corner for fixing the finished fountain to the wall.

3 Drill the holes to attach the wall pot, and those at each corner. Then, using a 16mm drill bit, drill the hole for the waterspout and the hole above the wall pot. Attach the wall pot securely to the board using stainless steel nuts and bolts.

4 Mix some of the blue colorizer with the adhesive, following the manufacturer's instructions. Mix up enough blue adhesive to cover the entire board and wall pot,

except the area occupied by the fish. Working quickly, smooth the coloured adhesive over the board and wall pot using a paint scraper, working up to the outline of the fish. Complete a section at a time, pushing marbles into the adhesive as you go to form curves rolling away from the body of the fish. Use a wet palette knife to smooth water unevenly over the surface to produce the mottled effect.

6 Place the mirror glass under a tea towel and use a small hammer to break it into fragments of around 2.5cm (1in). Butter the backs of the mirror fragments with tile adhesive and fill in the body of the fish. Work up to the hole for the spout, leaving the tail and fins undecorated.

7 Use tile nippers to shape some long shards of mirror glass, using the appropriate safety equipment (see page 25). Use the long shards to create the tail and fins, orientating the shards to emphasize the shapes.

8 Use a sponge or squeegee to push grout into the spaces between the fragments of mirror mosaic, working carefully up to the blue background. Wipe away any excess grout with a damp sponge, rinsing it out frequently to avoid leaving any streaks on the tiles.

9 Place the pump in the wall pot and attach the hose to it. Thread the hose and the electric cable through the hole above the pot to the back of the board. Cut the pipe to length and push it back through the hole in the mouth of the fish so that it is flush with the surface. Fix the pipe in position with silicone sealant.

10 Fill the wall pot with soap bubble marbles and glass shells, and then with water, and switch on the pump to check the flow.

11 Hang the completed fish fountain on either a wall or a fence, making sure that it is securely supported.

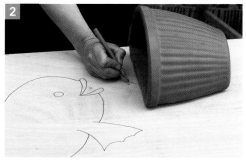

Water wheel

Set into an area of lush planting this shimmering water wheel makes a superb focal point surrounded by water-worn stones.

Plain, flat and drab, the surfaces of reproduction millstone water features almost demand to be embellished. The simplicity of the shape and the ease with which it becomes an impressive focal point make this an excellent project for the beginner. Bejeweled in glass mulch, the stone takes on a whole new character. The bold star design occupies the entire surface of the stone and keeps its appeal even when submerged. The glass mulch used to produce the design is tumbled to remove sharp edges and will survive unscathed underwater. A pump hidden in a reservoir under the millstone propels the frothing water over the decorated surface of the millstone. The reservoir could be simply a hole lined with a butyl pond liner, or a rigid plastic reservoir. Choose an adjustable pump, so a pleasing flow of water can be contrived.

SHOPPING LIST

1 millstone
concrete sealant
cement-based, waterproof tile adhesive
0.5kg blue glass mulch
1kg green glass mulch
pond liner with sand and an underlay or a
    rigid reservoir
1 adjustable pond pump
1 piece of water pipe
silicone sealant
2 x 20kg bags of green paddle stones or
    large cobbles

TOOLS

brush to apply sealant
chalk
colander
paint scraper or palette knife
spade

1 Clean and dry the millstone, then prime the surface with concrete sealant and allow to dry.

2 Use chalk to mark the star design on the millstone. The template on page 122 can be used as a guide.

3 Wash the glass mulch under running water in a colander to rinse off any dust and drain well. Leave the glass to dry before use.

4 Spread a small amount of adhesive, about a third the depth of the stones on edge, into the star area.

5 Push pieces of blue glass mulch set on edge into the adhesive bed. There should be enough adhesive to come about a third of the way up the fragments of glass, so that once pushed in they retain their character. Cram the fragments as close together as possible. Continue until the whole star is complete.

6 Spread some more adhesive into one of the areas between the points of the star.

7 In the same way as step 5, fill in the background with green glass mulch, working up to the edges of the stone.

8 Make a reservoir by digging a hole and installing a pond liner, which should rest on sand and an underlay, or a rigid plastic tank. Fill it up with water and place the pump in it.

9 Sit the millstone over the reservoir containing the pump. Push the hose from the pump into the hole of the millstone so that it is just flush with the surface of the stone and, if necessary, use silicone sealant to hold it in place.

10 Before finally positioning the stone, adjust the flow of the water until you are happy with it.

11 When you are happy with the flow, surround the water wheel with large paddle stones.

IDEAS TO INSPIRE

• You could try a pronounced spiral design executed in glass mulch; it would suit the watery theme and the circular shape of the millstone.

• For a really quick fix, complete just the blue star motif, leaving the rest of the surface undecorated. The contrast between the glittering glass and matt concrete will be attractive, and, if the water feature becomes tiresome, you can finish it.

• Other materials could work well. Florist's beads would produce a similar glassy effect, while the rounded pebbles of aquatic gravels destined for aquariums should produce something with a more rustic, earthy feel.

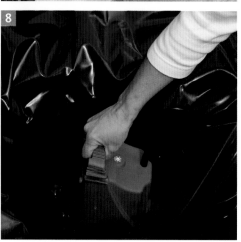

DECORATIVE TIP

Surround the water feature with lush foliage for a natural effect. Choose leafy plants such as ferns, hostas and rodgersias.

WALL
DECORATIONS

An expanse of bare wall or fence is perhaps the most obvious and tempting garden surface to decorate – a conspicuous, inviting blank canvas. A plain wall is at best uninteresting and at worst oppressive and unattractive. Mosaic is the ideal solution for shady, colourless places, bringing colour, interest and sparkle that will last all year round. That is not to say, however, that sunny hospitable walls cannot be given an inspiring lift with a well-chosen mosaic.

There are a number of ways wall decoration can be approached: the first is to apply the decoration directly onto the surface. This relies upon the surface of the wall being sound and means that the mosaic is a reasonably permanent addition to the garden. The second is to build the mosaic design on a backing, marine plywood for example, and then mount this on the wall or fence. This produces a fantastically mobile piece that can be moved around the garden as often as you like. For really ambitious projects, the piece may have to be worked as a series of smaller, manageable panels that can be hung together. Small panels of decoration are usually the only option for fences and trellises that cannot support a great weight and whose surfaces are too mobile or uneven to allow mosaic to be applied directly.

Producing a mosaic picture is the most obvious way to cheer up a drab expanse of wall, but there are alternatives. Mosaic-framed mirrors make a wonderful decoration for shady corners, reflecting light back into the garden. A large mirror can be decorated artfully and positioned to make it look like a doorway through to a garden beyond. These faux doorways or windows can create an illusion of space and a sense of mystery.

Quick and easy to create, a mosaic border or frieze is an equally effective wall decoration. A strip of mosaic, however narrow, has real impact and is a useful device for changing the proportions of an expanse of wall.

Backing materials must be durable and sturdy enough to support the weight of the mosaic. Timber should be exterior grade and sealed with PVA. Choose metal fixings that will not corrode or they may stain the mosaic. Any materials that will withstand the elements can be used for wall decorations, so be adventurous.

Left: **The lavishly decorated walls of these stairs make them immensely inviting. A collection of colourful ceramic tiles clothe the walls in pattern. The 'worn in' character of the decoration softens it and only adds to its charm.**

Right: **A bold mosaic of broken ceramics almost entirely covers the walls of this Australian house and garden. The vibrant colours and attention-grabbing design dominate the area and is tempered only by a scattering of simple architectural plants.**

Faux window

Nestled amongst lush foliage, this cleverly placed mirror creates the illusion of a tantalizing garden beyond.

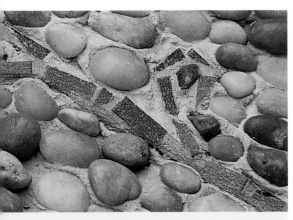

SHOPPING LIST

1 arched-topped mirror suitable for use
   outdoors
50 green glass mosaic tiles
grey cement-based tile adhesive
70 green 'gemme' mosaic tiles
1 kg (2 lb) aquatic gravel
grey cement-based grout

TOOLS

felt tip pen
tile nippers
small palette knife
paint scraper
damp sponge
dry cloth

The mirror is framed in subtle materials so that, at first glance, it is less obvious than the mysterious garden reflected in it. The beautifully rounded, tactile pebbles used to create the frame are a great foil for the glass mosaic tiles that make up the vine winding loosely around it.

The ability to bounce light back into the garden makes this mirror perfect for brightening a dark corner, making the space lighter and seemingly larger. The skill here is in mounting the mirror so that it is most often seen from an angle at which the garden is reflected in it, rather than the individual admiring the view. Mounting mirrors on sunny walls has to be done with care, as the mirror will reflect the sun's rays back and could be uncomfortable and hurt your eyes. Choose a mirror larger than the window you want to create, as the frame is applied on top of the glass. Opt for a mirror with pre-drilled holes to make mounting easy.

1 Use a felt tip pen to draw the frame design onto the mirror. Add the stalks, leaves and tendrils of the vine, allowing some of them to overlap onto what will be the window. The template on page 123 can be used as a rough guide.

2 Use tile nippers to nip the green glass mosaic tiles into strips to form the stalks and tendrils. Butter each piece with adhesive and, following the lines of the design, apply the strips to the mirror leaving space for grout between pieces.

3 Cut the 'gemme' tiles into random pieces and apply them in the same way to form the vine leaves. Continue until the whole vine is complete.

4 Wash the small pebbles thoroughly and leave them to dry. Spread a small section of the frame with adhesive and push the pebbles into the adhesive bed in orderly rows, all orientated in the same direction, following the curve of the mirror. Work right up to the vine and the edges of the frame. Avoid the pre-drilled mounting holes. Allow the adhesive to dry.

5 When the adhesive is dry, mix up enough grout to fill the spaces between the pieces of tile making up the vine.

6 Use a paint scraper to spread it over the whole of the vine, filling all the gaps between the tiles and working carefully up to the edges of the embedded pebbles.

7 Wipe the surface of the tiles with a damp sponge to remove any excess grout, rinsing it frequently. Finally, when the grout is almost dry, polish the whole frame and mirror with a dry cloth.

Stained glass sun panel

When back-lit by the sun, this stained glass panel will glow, projecting coloured pools of light onto the garden around it.

IDEAS TO INSPIRE

• The panel could be left without grout to produce a much lighter, airier piece.
• A series of panels, each worked in a different colour of glass, mounted along a stretch of trellis would make an exciting display.
• Florist's beads could be used in the place of or in combination with the bottle fragments. They are available in a vast range of colours and would give a greater choice, although their thickness means that they let less light through than bottle glass.

Even without direct sunlight, the panel's attractive patchwork of reflective glass will catch the eye. The coloured glass used to produce stained glass windows can be expensive, but here a collection of brightly coloured mineral water and wine bottles and mirror glass has been recycled to great effect. The bottles are smashed and then shaped with tile nippers into roughly uniform pieces. The pieces are mounted on a clear glass panel using a clear silicone sealant to let the light shine through.

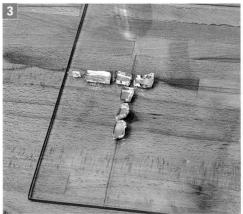

1 Using the template on page 123 as guide, mark out the design on a piece of paper. Place the paper under the sheet of glass and trace the design onto the surface of the glass using a felt tip pen and ruler.

2 Place the mirror glass under a tea towel and smash it using a small hammer. Wear protective clothing (see page 26) as breaking glass produces flying shards.

3 Use tile nippers to shape the fragments into elongated rectangles. One by one, spread the backs of the pieces with silicone sealant and firmly push them into place on the glass panel to form the framework of the design.

4 Cover the glass bottles with a tea towel and hit them with a hammer to break them into small pieces.

5 Nip the fragments of bottle into roughly rectangular pieces of an even size. It is far easier to produce all of the fragments for one section before starting to apply them.

6 Use a gloved finger to spread one panel of the design with a thin layer of silicone sealant. Push pieces of the glass into the sealant in rows for a neat effect.

7 Repeat this with each of the panels until the design is complete and allow to dry.

8 When the silicone is dry, use a squeegee to spread grout over the surface of the panel, forcing grout into the spaces between the shards of glass to form even grout joints.

9 Use a damp sponge to remove any excess grout from the surface of the glass, rinsing it out in clean water from time to time. When the grout is almost dry, polish the glass with a dry cloth.

DECORATIVE TIP

The curved surfaces of the bottles mean that the fragments of glass have to be small. Buying sheets of coloured glass would give the freedom to use larger pieces to complete the project. Stained glass is easily cut in the same way as tiles using a tile cutter and comes in a fantastic array of colours.

Before deciding which glass or bottles to use, check their colour with light shining through them. Some seemingly promising glass can look a very different shade when it is lit.

Moorish frieze

Inspired by the mosaic tradition of Morocco, this fresh, uncomplicated frieze is evocative of warmer climes.

DECORATIVE TIP

This simple frieze could be used to frame doors and windows, or to define panels, as well as dividing an expanse of wall into sections.

Small strips of pattern and colour can have a disproportionately large impact on the feel of a space and go a long way to establishing a warm, exotic mood, yet friezes take relatively little time to create. A continuous frieze around part of the garden will give it unity; therefore a frieze can be a useful device to strengthen the character or style of an area.

Friezes can be composed of a whole range of different materials, and can be designed to enhance any mood. If the walls are flat, reasonably even and the materials chosen permit, the indirect mosaic method can be used to produce manageable interlocking sections of border on a more convenient flat surface, that can then be transferred to the wall. On uneven surfaces or when using irregular materials, the frieze should be applied directly to the wall.

1 Using a pencil and a ruler, draw a line about 45cm (18in) long on the matt side of the brown paper – this is a manageable length for a section of frieze. This will be the centre line for the design. The template on page 124 will be helpful.

2 Apply some water-soluble glue to the brown paper and start to build up the design. Begin by placing white tiles face down and corner to corner along the central line.

3 Use the white tiles as a guide to position the green tiles, leaving a consistent, small gap between them. Leave one end of the section of frieze so that it will interlock with the beginning of the next.

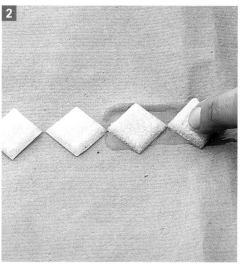

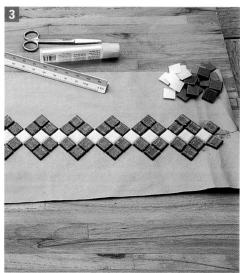

4 Use a paint scraper to apply grout to the frieze, working it into the spaces between the tiles. Applying the grout at this stage prevents the adhesive from squashing on to the fronts of the tiles. Clean all excess grout from the backs of the tiles. Trim the paper.

5 Apply a thin layer of adhesive to the back of the frieze, enough for the tiles to bed into but not so much as to push out when the frieze is pressed into position on the wall.

6 Firmly push the frieze into place on the wall. Remove any adhesive that oozes out immediately. Repeat with all the sections of the frieze until it is complete, taking care to interlock the sections accurately and keep it level.

7 When the adhesive is dry, moisten the brown paper with a wet sponge and gently peel the paper away to reveal the frieze. Carefully reposition any tiles that may have come away with the paper, and repair any areas of grout as necessary. Finally polish off the mosiac with a soft cloth.

FRIEZE VARIATIONS

Top left: Evocative of days spent on the beach, this unusual frieze is made up of a collection of shells applied straight to the wall. The frieze could even include pieces of driftwood. Here the shells have been worked in a straight line, but they could be arranged in a gently undulating band. This type of frieze would be great for a seaside garden and could be placed at any height on the wall.

Below left: Natural, rounded pebbles applied directly to the wall make a very simple but attractively textured surface decoration. Each of the tactile pebbles has been buttered with adhesive and pushed into position. The frieze can be made quickly and easily. Don't be tempted to use large pebbles as the effect would be too coarse, but the stream of small pebbles could be widened to increase its impact.

Top right: The geometric pattern of these mirror tiles will add a touch of glitter to any wall. Reflecting all that is around it, this frieze is like a band of pure light hung around the garden. Its glitzy character is probably only suited to the most contemporary and daring of outdoor spaces however.

Below right: A ribbon of vivid blue glass tiles makes an appealing border created in the same way as the Moorish frieze. The simple design and harmonious colours create a subtle effect.

Make up your own design for a frieze or use any of the templates for the designs featured here on page 124.

FURNITURE

Applying mosaic to a piece of garden furniture can effect a magical transformation: an inexpensive, worn or mundane piece can become something stylish and unique. In any garden designed to be lived in and enjoyed, furniture plays an important role – a shaded bench to relax on, a single chair in a sunny spot for lounging or a table for alfresco dining. The role of furniture, however, can go beyond the practical. A decorative piece can contribute much to the structure of the garden, creating an architectural or colourful accent amidst the foliage. A beautiful bench or small table and chairs, for example, might become the attention-grabbing focal point that draws the eye along a vista, while a brightly decorated table can be used to add a burst of colour to a drab, grey terrace. Mosaic furniture can be a permanent feature in a garden's design or a moveable feast placed where it is needed, either to be used or to just look good.

Above: The regular curves of this stunning Gaudi bench are lavishly decorated with a mosaic of broken ceramic tiles.

Left: Bright and cheery, the simple repeated geometric design of this tabletop would add a welcome splash of colour to the garden.

Opposite: In a garden rich in mosaic, this unusual take on a garden seat looks quite at home with its almost chintzy decoration.

Fortunately, many readily available mosaic materials make fantastically durable surfaces that are easy to keep clean. This makes them ideally suited for garden furniture, which has not only to look good but also to work hard. Glazed ceramics are good; both tiles and broken crockery work well and offer a choice of colour. Glass mosaic tiles have similar qualities and can be used to produce a more luxurious effect. Use a grout sealant to protect the grout on tabletops from ugly stains and grease.

Tabletops are the most obvious surfaces to decorate, but it is possible to decorate chairs and benches – although, without the addition of a few cushions, the result may work better as a piece of outdoor art rather than a comfortable seat.

Any piece of furniture must be prepared thoroughly before the mosaic decoration is applied. Surfaces should be completely dry, sound and if necessary primed with diluted PVA glue. Tabletops are usually best tackled by firmly screwing a piece of marine plywood to the surface, to give a stable flat surface to work on. A dressing of mosaic, perhaps coupled with a coat of exterior paint or woodstain, can transform a piece of furniture designed for use inside into one perfect for the garden. Searching out inexpensive pieces in junk shops and giving them a new identity with mosaic can be a fantastic way to furnish your garden in your own personal style at very little cost.

Mosaic is also a great way to add a colourful gloss to simply constructed homemade furniture. Shelves for displaying collections of small plants and *objets trouvés*, stools and simple benches are not only useful but easy to construct. If you just add a slick dressing of mosaic, their basic construction will be disguised.

Citrus dining table

A combination of whole, cut and randomly broken tiles creates a lively design on this zesty, citrus dining table.

SHOPPING LIST

For a table 88 x 88cm (35½ x 35½in) square

1 sheet of 1.8cm (¹¹⁄₁₆in) thick marine plywood

PVA glue

stainless steel screws

cream woodstain

4 pieces of wooden batten, about 0.5 x 5cm (³⁄₁₆ x 2in) in profile and 88cm (35½in) long

14 orange, 17 yellow and 10 terracotta coloured ceramic tiles

cement-based tile adhesive

panel pins

white cement-based grout

TOOLS

saw

sandpaper

paintbrush

drill and drill bit

screwdriver

paintbrush

pencil

ruler

tile cutter

tile nippers

palette knife

tea towel

small hammer

grouting squeegee

damp sponge

dry cloth

The brightly coloured mosaic top on the table has been coupled with a coat of fresh cream woodstain on the table legs and the chairs to transform an uninspiring dining set into a desirable centrepiece for alfresco dining. A handful of resilient ceramic tiles are used to construct the geometric pattern. Without the panels of randomly smashed tile fragments, the design would be rather predictable and flat.

The top of this table, like many outdoor tables, is made up of several pieces of wood, so a sheet of marine plywood is mounted on the tabletop to provide a secure base for the design.

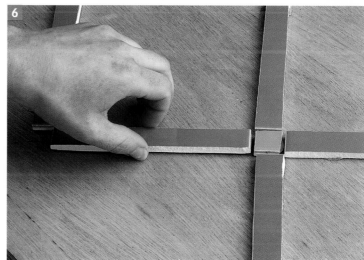

1. Cut the plywood to the exact size of the tabletop and sand off any rough edges. Seal the plywood with PVA glue diluted in equal quantities with water and leave to dry. Stain the table and batten and leave to dry.

2. Drill a hole at each corner of the board and securely screw it to the tabletop so that there is no movement.

3. Use a pencil and ruler to mark out the diagonal grid of the design on the board. Use the template on page 125 as a guide.

4. Using a tile cutter, score and snap enough 1.5cm (⁹⁄₁₆in) wide strips of terracotta tile to create the main grid of the pattern. It may help to lay the pieces out on the design as you cut them to ensure you cut the correct quantity.

5. To make the orange squares that form part of the grid, make strips from the orange tiles using the tile cutter, then nip these into squares using the tile nippers. It does not matter if there is some irregularity in the shapes that you cut – it will not detract from the finished effect.

6. Now, working from the centre of the tabletop, butter each strip or square of tile individually and push it firmly into place on the board. Check as you go that the whole and half tiles will fit neatly into the squares being formed, with just a small space for the grout.

7. Next, use the tile cutter to cut some yellow tiles in half by scoring a diagonal line across the tile from corner to corner and snapping them. Add the half and whole tiles to the design by buttering each piece and pushing it into place.

8 Check that the surface of the mosaic is level, then add a border of strips of orange tile around the mosaic to the edges of the tabletop.

9 Place the remaining yellow tiles under a tea towel and smash them using a small hammer. Spread a bed of adhesive in the remaining squares of the design, one by one, and push the fragments of tile into place. Try to achieve an approximate fit between the pieces and ensure that the grout spaces are not too large. Leave to dry.

10 Tack the lengths of wood around the top of the table so the top of the wood is flush with the top of the mosaic. This neatly disguises the cut edges of the tiles, and the join between the table and the board.

11 Mix up enough white grout to finish the whole surface, and, using a squeegee, spread it over the surface of the mosaic, pushing the grout into the spaces between the tiles.

12 Clean off the excess grout with a damp sponge to leave neat seams flush with the surface of the tiles. Rinse the sponge frequently and allow the grout to dry. Finally, polish off the mosaic with a dry cloth. Grout sealant can be used to prevent grout becoming stained.

IDEAS TO INSPIRE

• The same design could be repeated on the seats of the chairs on a similar plywood base, but cushions would be needed for long leisurely lunches!

• Leftover plywood and tiles could be used to make matching trivets or heat mats to protect the table from hot serving dishes.

• To create a cool, calm dining area, you could complete the same design in harmonious shades of blue.

DECORATIVE TIP

The design is easily scaled up or down to fit any size of tabletop. The width of the border can be increased or decreased so that a grid of whole tiles can be used.

Succulent display shelves

This novel set of shelves makes an exceptional display for three small succulents in simple pots.

An exuberant mosaic façade of blue and white ceramics and fragments of mirror masks the basic construction of the homemade shelves, which require very little skill to complete. The architectural shape of the small succulents lends itself to this kind of treatment and the greyish bloom of their leaves tones well with the blue and white theme, but any small plant could be given significance by being exhibited in this way. A splash of silver paint on the plain pots produces a calming note that balances the rather chaotic mosaic.

SHOPPING LIST

1 sheet of 1.8cm (¹¹⁄₁₆in) thick marine
    plywood at least 30 x 75cm (12 x 30in)
PVA glue
18cm (7in) tanalized fence post, 15cm (6in)
    square in profile
6 stainless steel screws
mirror glass
cement-based tile adhesive
blue and white crockery (about 5–6 plates)
grey cement-based grout
3 small pots painted silver
3 small succulents

TOOLS

saw
paintbrush
ruler
pencil
drill and drill bit
tea towel
small hammer
palette knife

1 Cut the plywood into a rectangle 35 x 75cm (14 x 30in) and seal it on both sides and its edges with PVA glue diluted in equal quantities with water. Use a ruler and pencil to mark out three 6cm (2½in) lengths of fence post and cut them off as squarely as possible using a hand saw.

2 Arrange the three blocks of wood on the plywood and, when you are satisfied with the arrangement, mark their positions on the board. Drill two holes set diagonally in the board for each block and then screw them securely into place. It is important the blocks do not move or the surface of the mosaic may crack.

3 Use a pencil and ruler to mark the position of the mirrored panel behind each shelf. Place the mirror under a tea towel and break it with a hammer into fragments about 2cm (¾in) long (see pages 26–7) .

4 Taking great care, butter the backs of the fragments one by one with adhesive and fill in the panels.

5 Break the blue and white crockery in the same manner as the mirror. Spread a small area of the board with a bed of adhesive and push the china pieces into position. Repeat this until the whole structure is covered.

6 When the adhesive is dry, mix up the grout and use a sponge to force it into the gaps. The surface is likely to be uneven as crockery is being used, but make the joints as neat as possible. Wipe away any excess grout with a damp sponge, rinsing out the sponge frequently. When the grout is dry, buff the mosaic with a dry cloth.

IDEAS TO INSPIRE

• The shelves are also perfect for holding candles. The flickering flames are reflected in the mirror panels to great effect.
• Pretty yellow violas in yellow pots would look charming exhibited on a similar shelf decorated with dainty pink, yellow and blue bone china.
• The shelf can be made whatever shape or size you fancy.

DECORATIVE TIP

When using a mixture of broken china, it is best to break all the china you intend to use and mix the fragments so that no one pattern or shade of blue dominates an area of the design. The finished piece will also look neater if the pieces are approximately the same size.

Butler's tray table

Given a wash of translucent woodstain and a panel of opulent mosaic, a butler's tray table is a perfect garden table.

Whether it holds a cooling drink by a deckchair or a few items at a barbecue, a small practical table that can be brought out when needed, then folded and stowed away, is a valuable addition to the garden. The sumptuous, rich purple 'gemme' tiles shot with sparkling metal are a real indulgence, but a few go a long way. Using just a small number engenders a feeling of luxury, making the table a treat to use. The geometric design can easily be scaled up or down.

The solid, flat base of the tray table means that the mosaic decoration can be applied directly to its base; if the tray is slatted or uneven, treat it like the Citrus Dining Table (see pages 76–9).

SHOPPING LIST
For a 33 x 49cm (13 x 19½in) table)
1 small folding table
1 sheet of brown parcel paper
water-soluble gum or PVA glue
128 white glass mosaic tiles
200 purple 'gemme' mosaic tiles
grey cement-based tile adhesive
grey cement-based grout

TOOLS
ruler
pencil
notched comb
scissors
damp sponge
grouting squeegee
dry cloth

1 Measure the tabletop and use a pencil to draw a rectangle of exactly the same size on the matt side of the brown paper. Mark the centre point and draw a grid of squares onto the paper, working from the centre. The squares should be slightly larger than the mosaic tiles to allow for grouting. Use the pencil to colour code different areas of the design using the template on page 125.

2 Use water-soluble glue to stick the mosaic pieces to the brown paper face down, following the pattern. Leave the glue to dry.

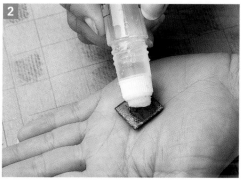

3 Use a small notched comb to apply a thin, even bed of adhesive to the surface of the table, ensuring the whole surface is covered.

4 Cut the excess paper away from around the mosaic.

5 Starting at one end, lower it into position on the tabletop, tile side down.

6 Press it firmly into place over the whole mosaic. Leave to dry.

7 Use a damp sponge to moisten the brown paper and, after a few minutes, gently peel it away. If any of the tiles come away with the brown paper, use adhesive to glue them back into place.

8 Mix up enough grout to complete the project and use a squeegee to spread grout over the surface of the mosaic. Use a damp sponge to remove any excess grout from the surface of the tiles and finally, when the grout is almost dry, use a dry cloth to polish off the surface.

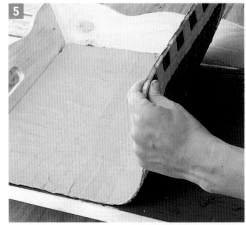
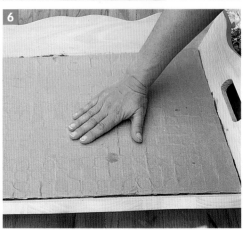

IDEAS TO INSPIRE

• This project would look chic scaled up to decorate a smart dining table, with each mosaic tile being replaced by a block of four or nine similarly coloured mosaic tiles for a really luxurious, opulent effect.

• To give the table a Mediterranean feel, try using blue and yellow glass tiles to create the mosaic and paint the table with a vibrant blue woodstain.

• If you have a favourite place to sit and relax in the garden, complete the design with colours that will complement or harmonize with the planting.

PATHS AND
STEPPING STONES

Paths are a practical part of any garden design. Their prime function is to allow easy movement around the garden in all weathers, but their importance goes beyond this – often they divide the garden, defining different areas. They can lead the eye towards points of interest and change the pace at which anyone strolls around the garden, encouraging them to take a prescribed route. A set of well-designed paths can be the threads that hold a plan together and should be given as much thought as any other part of a garden's structure.

Incorporating a pattern into the surface of the path by using a number of different materials is a great way to give it character. In general, the path should be in harmony with its surroundings, reflecting the mood of the spaces through which it passes. The materials you choose, the pattern you create with them and the route the path takes will all play a part in creating the character of the path. There is plenty of choice when it comes to selecting materials, but practical as well as aesthetic considerations should guide your final decision. Some paths are the main routes through the garden; the surface of these paths must stand up to constant use and be immensely practical, wide and level enough for wheelbarrows and wheeled toys if required. Other paths can be a little more frivolous and sacrifice a little practicality for the benefit of good looks. That is not to say that durability and good looks are mutually exclusive.

Bricks, paving blocks, paving slabs, timber, concrete, gravel, glass mulch and even crushed shells can be used to construct paths. Choose solid paving materials for a level path, such as bricks or paving slabs; they can be combined to create formal or more random patterns. Using a loose material, such as gravel or glass, as part of design makes the path much less even and more difficult to walk on. It is also worth considering how the material will look and behave when it is wet – some smooth stone slabs become very slippery and so would not be a wise choice for a main pathway.

The pattern you choose to decorate the path will have an effect on how long it appears and the speed at which you walk on it. If you choose a directional design, it will encourage haste and draw the eye quickly onwards; directional designs have lines that run along the length of the path. To slow the pace down, choose a design that runs across the path in bands. A path with a strong directional

Below left: **Packed closely together, logs set on end with a contrasting infill create a path suited to only light traffic.**

Below: **This hard-wearing path, composed of slabs of slate and rounded cobbles, is suited to areas that get heavy traffic.**

pattern is excellent for drawing the eye along a vista towards an attractive focal point or view. Informal, meandering paths are especially suited to loose materials such as gravel; trying to create any kind of pattern on a winding path can be difficult.

Stepping stones are not only a practical way to provide a route across a well-trodden or boggy lawn, they also add interest and perhaps a burst of colour to the garden floor. They can be used to break up the monotony of other garden surfaces such as gravel or act as a guide to encourage a particular route around the garden. Stepping stones are quicker and more straightforward to construct than a path, but their strength depends upon their being set on a sound level base. This need only be soil or sharp sand, but they may crack if you leave any room for movement or rocking.

Below: **This design is strongly directional, with the orientation of the bricks echoing that of the path.**

Right: **A crisp chequerboard of gravel and wood blocks makes a practical, durable and stylish surface.**

Flowerpot path

This charming informal path is quick and inexpensive to lay and has an established, weathered look from the outset.

SHOPPING LIST
hardcore
8cm (3in) deep edging boards
40cm (16in) pegs made from 5cm (2in)
  square timber
preserving woodstain
galvanized nails
bonsai pans or small flowerpots
1:4 wet mortar mix (see pages 32–3)
reclaimed red bricks
Cotswold gravel

TOOLS
stringline and pegs
spade
paintbrush
trowel
spirit level
club hammer

IDEAS TO INSPIRE

• Any bricks or paving blocks – new or reclaimed – could be used in the design. Perhaps you could choose a brick to match your house.
• The bonsai pans could be replaced with small flowerpots or larger pots cut down with an angle grinder.
• If you have plenty of flowerpots, the same diamond pattern could be made with pots alone.

The worn reclaimed bricks and mellow Cotswold gravel used in the path's construction allow it to settle comfortably into the garden. The unusual design also includes clusters of up-turned flowerpots, which look at home alongside the red brick and are quite apt for a garden path. The character of the path is perfectly suited to a cottage garden with borders billowing with an eclectic mix of plants, or perhaps a decorative potager.

The pattern is really only suited to straight paths – the diamond shapes would distort if the path were curved. The pattern has the effect of moving the eye along the path, but the punctuating groups of flowerpots help to reduce the speed at which the eye progresses.

Properly constructed, this path is hard-wearing enough to be a main thoroughfare but the loose and slightly uneven surface could make it difficult with a wheelbarrow and impossible for wheeled toys.

1 Mark out and prepare the base of the path (see pages 28–31) so that you have a firm base of compacted hardcore to work on. Stain the path-edging boards on both sides with preserving woodstain and allow to dry. Drive in the timber pegs at 1.5m (5ft) intervals along both sides of the path. Lay the edging boards on the inside edges of the pegs and nail them in place to form a continuous edge.

2 Fill the bonsai pans with mortar and leave them to dry. Set up a stringline along the centre of the path as a guide and lay out the bricks and pots to form the pattern, adjusting the positions and angles of the bricks until you are happy with the effect.

3 Lay a small bed of mortar for the first group of pots and push them in. Their surface should be 4–5cm (1½–2in) above the level of the hardcore – this will be the depth of the gravel. More than 5cm (2in) makes walking difficult, less and bare patches are likely to appear as the gravel moves. Use a spirit level to check that the pots are level.

4 Lay a bed of mortar for the bricks of the first diamond and push them into position. Use the handle of a club hammer to tap them into place. Check that the bricks are level with each other and with the flowerpots. To keep the bricks stable, pack the mortar around them to just below the top edge. Continue until the first length of path is complete, then move on to the next.

5 Taking care not to dislodge the bricks, fill the spaces of the design with gravel so that the surface of the gravel is flush with that of the bricks. Leave the path overnight before walking on it and a week before subjecting it to the heavier traffic of wheelbarrows and lawn mowers.

Mosaic slabs

These chic, stylish blue slabs really pep up a garden floor and look equally good set in gravel or grass or built into a patio.

SHOPPING LIST

concrete paving slabs, about 30cm
    (12in) square
concrete sealant
grey cement-based tile adhesive
193 glass mosaic tiles in two shades of blue
    – per slab
3 silver mosaic tiles – per slab
grey cement-based grout

TOOLS

paintbrush
paint scraper or palette knife
grouting squeegee
damp sponge
dry cloth

IDEAS TO INSPIRE

• Rather than using shades of blue, choose a colour to match your own colour scheme. With warmer colours such as oranges and reds, the silver tiles could be replaced by gold.
• The flat square surface provided by the paving stone has plenty of potential. A straightforward geometric design could be used to decorate the surface rather than a random mix of colours, or even something figurative. Remember that anything too fussy will lose its impact at a distance.

Blue glass mosaic tiles are beautifully smooth and reflective and a few silver tiles provide a brilliant, flashing accent that lifts the whole design. A real luxury, these silver tiles are made by sandwiching a layer of silver in clear glass. They come with either a smooth or rippled finish, and a small number is all you need to give a touch of sparkle.

The slabs are deceptively easy to make: an inexpensive concrete slab is dressed with a glamorous mosaic façade. Choose the least textured slabs available or work on the reverse if they are flatter. Glass mosaic stones are not only beautiful, but also practical – easily withstanding a good amount of wear.

1 Give the clean, dry paving stones a coat of concrete sealant.

2 Working on a small area at a time, spread adhesive onto the flattest face of the stone and push the mosaic tiles into the bed of adhesive in neat rows. It may be helpful to draw some guidelines onto the face of the paving stone. Choose the tiles at random and include just one or two silver tiles on each stone.

3 When the adhesive is dry, mix some grey grout and use a squeegee to squeeze it into the spaces between the tiles until one continuous smooth surface is formed. Use a damp sponge to remove the grout from the surface of the tiles. Rinse the sponge repeatedly to avoid smearing the surface of the mosaic.

4 After 10–15 minutes, polish off the surface of the tiles with a soft dry cloth to remove any surface dust. As soon as the grout is completely dry the stones can be put into the garden.

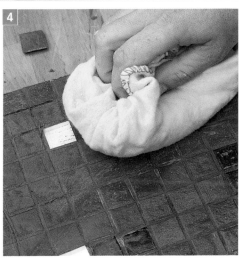

Fern pattern stones

The fossil-like impressions in the surface of these paving stones capture the elegant tracery of arching fern fronds.

SHOPPING LIST

5 x 1cm (2 x ⅜in) timber battens (the lengths depends on the size of the frame)
nails
plastic sheeting or bin bags
1:3 wet mortar mix (see pages 32–3)
wire mesh (optional)
fern fronds

TOOLS

saw
hammer
spade
builder's float

IDEAS TO INSPIRE

• Almost anything can be used to create impressions in the mortar – bark, twigs, twine, rope and shells are all worth a try.
• To add a splash of colour, the stones could be painted with masonry paint or, alternatively, a colorant could be added to the mortar.

DECORATIVE TIP

Ferns make an excellent impression because there is plenty of fine detail to be captured in the imprint, but other foliage might be equally successful. Leaves with attractive shapes, like those of *Acer* or even oak, are worth experimenting with to create a flurry of leaves across the surface of the paving stones.

Set into gravel or a swathe of grass, these stones make an unusual informal pathway with a surprisingly natural character. The colour of the sand used in the mortar mix will determine the final colour of the paving stones, so ask the advice of your supplier or experiment to find a colour that appeals. Buy enough sand to finish the whole batch of slabs, to guarantee a more or less consistent shade. Cast in basic wooden frames, the paving stones are produced by a reliable, straightforward method that takes no time at all to master.

1 Make a number of simple frames by nailing together four lengths of timber batten. The frames can be any size you wish, but using two or three sizes adds to the informality of the finished path. Place the frames on plastic sheeting or bin liners.

2 Fill the frames with mortar. For areas of heavy wear, it is advisable to sandwich a layer of wire mesh in the mix about halfway up.

3 Even out the surface of the mortar and use a damp builder's float to smooth it

out. Hold the float flat on the surface and slowly move it across with an even pressure. It takes only a little practice to master the technique.

4 Once the surface is smooth, gently press the fern fronds onto the mortar, ensuring that every piece of the frond is pushed down. Retain the natural curve of the frond as it is more likely to stay on the surface without moving than if you try to straighten it out. Repeat until all of the frames are filled. After a few minutes, go back and check that the ferns are still in contact with the mortar.

5 After three or four hours, gently start to peel away one of the fronds. If the impression remains firm, the ferns can be gently removed. If the impression fades or is watery, wait another couple of hours and try again.

6 Leave the paving stones overnight and then tap away the frames. Though solid, the mortar takes several days to reach full strength, so wait a week before installing the stones in the garden.

Pebble stepping stones

Miniature squares of pebble mosaic, just big enough for a single foot, make a conspicuous and practical pathway.

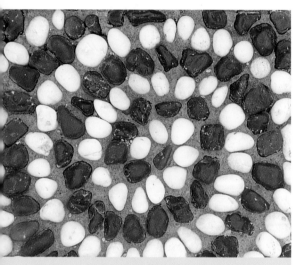

The smooth, rounded pebbles that make up the design are tightly packed together to form a hard-wearing surface that will stand up to the worst extremes of the weather and keep its good looks. The surface may appear slightly uneven and knobbly but it is comfortable to walk on, even in bare feet.

On a small surface, it is best to choose designs with simple lines – attempting too much detail on this tiny area would look cluttered. Here the strong contrast of black and white pebbles defines the bold motifs.

SHOPPING LIST

5x1cm (2x⅜in) timber battens (4 pieces 31cm (12¼in) long for each frame)
nails
plastic sheeting or bin bags
1:3 wet mortar mix (see pages 32–3)
black and white pebbles, about 4cm (1½in) across
1:3 dry mortar mix (see pages 32–3)

TOOLS

saw
hammer
trowel
plank of wood
mallet
brush
watering can with fine rose

1 Construct a number of simple frames like those used on pages 92–3. Use one of the frames as a guide to work out your design, squeezing in as many pebbles as possible so that the frame is packed full.

2 Place one of the frames on plastic sheeting or a bin bag and fill to just under halfway with mortar. Roughly level it off using a small pointing trowel.

3 Starting from the centre, transfer the pebble design to the mortar-filled frame, leaving the pebbles slightly proud of the frame and packing them as close together as possible.

4 When the frame is full, lay a piece of flat wood across the surface of the pebbles and gently tap it with a mallet, tamping down the pebbles until they are flush with the top of the frame. If the mortar is pushed too far up the sides of the pebbles, use less for the next stone. Repeat the process until all the frames are full. Leave to harden overnight.

5 Brush the dry mortar into the gaps between the pebbles. Use just enough to achieve an even layer but not enough to obscure the rounded shape of the pebbles. Brush all the dry mix off the surface of the pebbles and very gently sprinkle water over the top, taking care not to splash the dry mortar onto the tops of the pebbles as it may stain. Leave the stepping stones overnight and then gently tap them out of the frames. The sand and cement mix will take about a week to reach full strength, and then the stones can be put into position, sunk flush with the grass, in the garden.

IDEAS TO INSPIRE

• Pebbles come in a vast range of colours, shapes and sizes, so it is worth experimenting with the different textures and effects that can be achieved with different combinations.

• The stepping stones can be any shape or size. Make your path distinctive and unusual by producing novel shapes.

• Pieces of slate, ceramic glass marbles or terracotta pot could be used in combination with the pebbles, using the same technique to produce a myriad of designs and quite different effects.

Decorative threshold

A decorative threshold beneath an archway or gate will mark the transition between one area of the garden and the next.

SHOPPING LIST

1 tanalized fence post, 15cm (6in) square in profile
hardcore
12 bricks
1:4 wet mortar mix (see pages 32–3)
2kg (4¼lb) blue glass mulch

TOOLS

tape measure
pencil
saw
stringline and pegs
spade
mallet
plank of wood

IDEAS TO INSPIRE

• The wooden blocks could be livened up with a coat of colourful woodstain.
• Try replacing the glass mulch with tiny pebbles to produce a natural, rustic effect.
• This combination of wood and glass mulch could easily be incorporated into the paving of a terrace or path.

Here sparkling fragments of glass contrast with the end grain of natural wood to produce a cheerful chequerboard with a contemporary feel, great for adding interest to the garden floor. Displaying the end grain of the timber exposes the fascinating curving patterns of the tree's growth rings and adds charm to the finished effect. The contrast of two such different materials gives the threshold real impact.

A line of reclaimed bricks frames the threshold, but any edging could be employed. The threshold can be constructed at ground level or built as a step up to further emphasize the sense of crossing a boundary.

1 Measure and mark out 8cm (3in) blocks along the length of the fence post. Use a hand saw to cut the blocks, making the cut surfaces as level as possible.

2 Mark out the area of the threshold, excavate the area and create a firm foundation of hardcore (see pages 28–31). Lay a single course of bricks on a bed of mortar to form a rectangular frame to fit the opening or gateway. Butt the bricks up close together, with a layer of mortar between them to hold them firm. Allow the mortar to dry overnight.

3 Spread a 2.5cm (1in) layer of mortar in the brick frame. Arrange the blocks on the bed of mortar; there is plenty of time to perfect the pattern so you can experiment with your design.

4 When you are happy with their positions, use a mallet to tap the blocks into place.

5 Lay a plank over the blocks and tap it with the mallet, tamping the blocks down until they with the brick edge.

6 Fill the gaps between the blocks with glass mulch so it is just below that of the blocks and is less likely to move around. Leave the threshold overnight before treading on it, and for a week before subjecting it to any heavy wear and tear.

PATIOS

A place to eat, relax and entertain, the patio lies at the heart of outdoor life. Not only is the patio the hub of activities, it is often the link between house and garden, the most visible garden feature from the house. The cost of constructing a patio is likely to be the largest single expenditure in any garden scheme, so there are many good reasons why it is worth spending time over the planning process to get it just right. The patio you create should not only be a practical, hard-working surface but a joy to the eye that makes a real contribution to the garden's appeal. Using unusual materials and a little imagination, wonderful patterns and textures can be woven into the surface to produce something really special.

However, you don't have to create a whole new patio to get stunning effects. Some of the projects in this chapter are designed to breathe new life into characterless paving by replacing some of the existing stones with mosaic blocks of texture and colour. There are plenty of materials to choose from, but if the patio is next to the house then the first concern is to select materials that are in sympathy with the house, and then the garden. From a practical perspective, paving materials have to be tough enough to stand up to some of the hardest wear in

Left: **Worked in two colours, the intricate patterns in this pebble surface frame the simple fountain.**

the garden, and they must be easy to keep clean and provide a reasonably non-slip covering. You will need to consider both colour and texture when making a choice. Look at samples of material where you intend to use them and check how a shower of rain will affect their appearance – a sleek, silver-grey paving can quickly become a miserable dark grey when wet.

Successfully combining materials is fundamental to the creation of patterned paving. As a rule, only two or at most three paving materials should be used; too many and the result can be jumbled and confusing. Materials need to be chosen together, on the basis of how they interact and the impression they produce when they are combined. Lay samples out side by side to check how they work together.

Bricks, pebbles, cobbles, terracotta tiles, concrete paving stones, paving blocks, granite sets and slabs of stone are all reliable choices, but don't be afraid to explore other less obvious options – glass mosaic tiles, terracotta pots, end grain wood, slate mulch, roof tiles or cast concrete fossils are possibilities that might be just the thing to give life to your design. Whichever materials you decide on and however strong they are, the longevity of the patio depends on the quality of the foundation they rest upon: skimping on any aspect of the groundwork will almost certainly result in cracks and instability in the surface (see pages 30–1).

Small, intimate patios nestled into some secluded corner of the garden are a real luxury, quite different in character from the sociable, communal patio area. These small, calm oases are the perfect spot for quiet reflection away from the bustle of the house, allowing you to enjoy the garden from a different perspective. As such they can afford to be a little less practical and a little more idiosyncratic. Plants such as thyme and camomile can be planted in their surface and materials can be a little more uneven as table and chairs give way to a bench or deck chair, so loose materials like slate and gravel can be used.

Right: **A simple, repeated motif decorates this luxurious, impressive pebble mosaic surface.**

Beaded centrepiece

A circle of sparkling glass beads and a matching pot create a sumptuous centrepiece for the patio.

This centrepiece is attractive in its own right, but, with the addition of the exotic potted palm (see pages 106–7), it is spectacular. The pot, of course, can be relocated when more floor space is needed. The glass beads make a surprisingly durable surface once they are bonded together to form the mosaic; the ample distribution of grout joints gives good grip to the potentially slippery surface. Making the frame out of fragments of the slabs that have been removed is not only a triumph of recycling but it also creates a strong link between the mosaic design and the surrounding patio.

SHOPPING LIST

hardcore
grey cement-based tile adhesive
1:4 wet mortar mix (see pages 32–3)
2 sheets of brown parcel paper
water-soluble gum or PVA glue
light and dark blue florist's beads
grey cement-based grout

TOOLS

pickaxe
spade
stringline and peg
lump hammer
builder's float
tape measure
pencil
scissors
small notched comb
large sponge
dry cloth

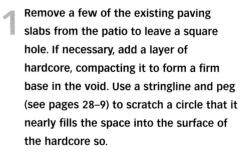

1 Remove a few of the existing paving slabs from the patio to leave a square hole. If necessary, add a layer of hardcore, compacting it to form a firm base in the void. Use a stringline and peg (see pages 28–9) to scratch a circle that it nearly fills the space into the surface of the hardcore so.

2 Use a lump hammer to break up some of the slabs you have removed. Working a small area at a time, lay a bed of adhesive around the outside of the circle and push in the fragments of slab so that their surfaces are flush with the surrounding paving. Continue until the border is complete.

3 The florist's beads are likely to be much shallower than the original paving, so add a screed of mortar over the hardcore. This also produces a firm base to work on. Use a wet builder's float to create a smooth, even surface about 1cm (⅜in) lower than the surrounding paving. It is important that the surface of the screed is as flat as possible.

4 Measure the diameter of the circle and use a pencil to draw two semi-circles of that diameter on the matt sides of the brown paper. As the mosaic is so large, it is much easier to make it in two halves.

Mark on the central disc of the sun motif. If you are also making the matching pot (see pages 106–7), make the central disc 2.5cm (1in) larger than the base of the pot so that it will show when the pot is in position. Mark the sunrays around the central disc, using the template on page 125 as a guide.

5 Starting from the centre, apply the glue to a section of the paper and build up the design by sticking concentric rings of florist's beads to the paper, curved side down. Leave a narrow gap between one bead and the next.

6 Use light blue beads for the sun and dark blue for the background. Continue applying the beads until the whole design is filled.

7 Cut away the excess brown paper from around the mosaic, cutting as close as possible to the beads. This will make it much easier to see what is going on when you come to lower the mosaic into position later.

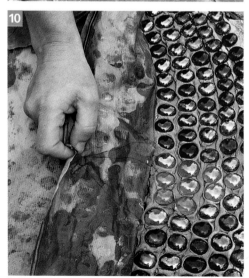

8 Using a small notched comb, apply a thin layer of adhesive to the screed in the circle. The layer needs to be as even as possible but not so deep as to rise too far up the sides of the beads when they are pushed into position. Take care not to scrape through the adhesive.

9 Line up the edge of one semi-circle of the mosaic, bead side down, and lower it little by little into position. Repeat this with the second semi-circle, taking care to line up the rows of beads on one half with those on the other. When you are happy with the position, push the beads firmly and evenly into the adhesive. Leave to dry.

10 Use a damp sponge to moisten the brown paper, leaving it for a few moments to let the adhesive dissolve.

Starting at one edge, carefully peel away the brown paper and use tile adhesive to replace any beads that peel away with the paper.

11 Mix up enough grout to finish the whole circle and, using a large sponge, spread the grout over the surface of the mosaic, pushing it into the gaps between the beads. The level of the grout should not obscure the shape of the beads, so push the sponge down around the beads.

12 Remove the excess grout with a clean, damp sponge, rinsing it frequently in clear water. Finally, when the grout is almost dry, polish the surface of the mosaic with a soft cloth. Leave to dry completely.

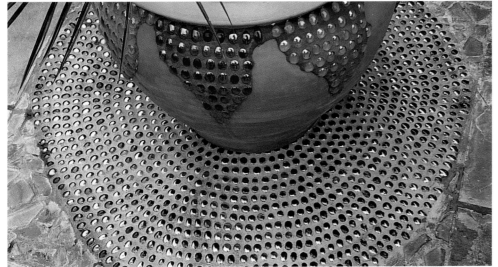

IDEAS TO INSPIRE

• The same centrepiece could be used to break up a straight stretch of path, temporarily arresting the eye.

• Try creating the circle as an eye-catching focal point at the end of a vista.

• The colourful, architectural arrangement could also be used as a focal point in an expanse of lawn or gravel.

Beaded palm pot

Embellished and planted with a palm, this pot combines with the beaded centrepiece to make an irrestistible focal point.

SHOPPING LIST

large terracotta pot
tracing paper
grey cement-based tile adhesive
light and dark blue florist's beads
grey cement-based grout

TOOLS

string
tape measure
pencil
palette knife
damp sponge
dry cloth

1 Ensure that the surface of the pot is clean, dry and dust free. Measure the neck of the pot. (The easiest way to do this is by wrapping a piece of string around the neck and measuring the string.) Calculate the width of the rays to give a whole number of rays around the rim of the pot.

2 Use a pencil to draw a single sunray on to a piece of tracing paper (using the tempate on page 125 as a guide), extending the sides at the top to the required width. Turn the piece of tracing paper over and shade over the lines with a pencil. Hold the tracing paper in position on the pot, shaded side down, and trace over the pencil lines, pressing firmly so that the design is transferred to the pot. Repeat all the way round the pot.

3 One by one, butter the backs of the florist's beads with adhesive and push them onto the pot in the marked areas. Organize them in rows and orientate them in the same direction. Alternate between light and dark blue rays as you move around the pot.

4 Mix up enough grey grout to finish the whole pot, making it a little stiffer than usual so it is more controllable. Use a sponge to apply the grout between

IDEAS TO INSPIRE

• Florist's beads are available in an incredible array of colours – deep reds, yellows, greens, pinks, orange and even black – so you can easily match the colours of your centrepiece to the character and planting of your patio.
• If the height of a palm is too imposing, use a low-growing, evergreen grass in the pot. The shaggy blue tufts of *Festuca glauca* 'Elijah Blue' would work well with the blue colour scheme.
• On a shady patio, an architectural evergreen fern, such as *Polystichum setiferum*, could take the place of the palm.

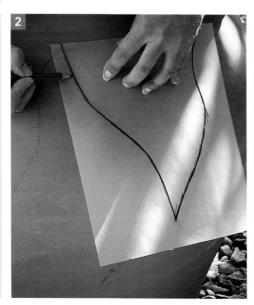

the beads, avoiding the bare terracotta. Finish the edges of the mosaic off neatly with grout, using a small palette knife if it is easier. Use a clean, damp sponge to remove any excess grout from the surface of the beads, rinsing it frequently. When the grout is almost dry, buff up the beads with a dry cloth.

5 Plant the pot with an elegant date palm and sit it at the centre of the mosaic floor. Take care not to drag the pot over the surface of the mosaic as it may scratch. Raise the pot slightly by standing it on pieces of tile tucked discreetly underneath to ensure good drainage. Here the pot has been mulched with grey slate to echo the slate of the patio.

DECORATIVE TIP

The pot is, of course, attractive in its own right and could easily be used alone without the patio centrepiece to stand it on.

Patterns in slate

These bold blocks of deep plum slate can add a strong, contemporary feel to a dated patio.

Pieces of slate mulch, set on edge, have been densely packed to produce a richly textured, striated surface – an excellent contrast to the relative flat featureless patio. The strong blocks of colour are set off effectively by the surrounding buff-coloured paving. The slate mulch has been arranged in one direction to give a simple but powerful effect, but it could be placed diagonally or in a variety of directions in the same panel to produce a pattern. If you try this, keep the pattern simple. Slate mulch is available in a range of colours, from plum through green to blue and grey, so you can choose the colour that suits your patio. The success of the effect relies on packing the slate as tightly as you possibly can. Use a large grade of mulch, with pieces up to 10cm (4in) in diameter, as this will be easier to work with.

SHOPPING LIST
hardcore
1:3 dry mortar mix (see pages 32–3)
slate mulch with 5–10cm (2–4in) pieces

TOOLS
pickaxe
spade
mallet
brush
watering can with fine rose

1 Remove one of the existing paving slabs from the patio and clear away any loose rubble from the hole. If necessary, create a firm base of compacted hardcore. Spread a layer of dry mortar mix in the hole so that is just under half full, and firm it down.

2 Push the pieces of slate into the dry mortar, arranging them on their edges. Make sure that each piece has a flat surface uppermost, and pack the pieces in as closely together as possible. Start by completing a row of slate at one side of the hole and then create a similar row at the opposite side in order to ensure a neat finish all round.

3 Now fill in the centre of the hole, working in rows and neatly interlocking each row with the one before it. To get a really tight fit it may be necessary to use a mallet to gently tap some of the pieces home. Keep the surface as level as possible and flush with the surrounding patio. Continue until the whole area is tightly packed with slate.

4 Next brush some dry mortar mix over the surface of the slate to partially fill any gaps or cracks. Be sparing with the dry mix or the texture of the surface will be obscured. Check that all the mortar is brushed off the surface of the slate and use a watering can with a fine rose to water the dry mix in gently. Leave to dry thoroughly before use.

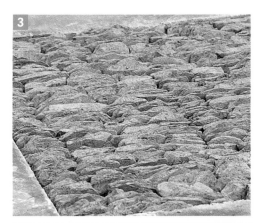

Chequerboard detail

Chunky black stable blocks and brilliant white gravel combine to create a strong geometric pattern.

SHOPPING LIST
hardcore
4 stable or paving blocks per detail
1:4 wet mortar mix (see pages 32–3)
white gravel

TOOLS
bolster chisel
club hammer
small builder's trowel
spirit level

The sturdy, solid and dark stable blocks contrast with the angular, radiant chips of stone, making a combination that is extreme but effective. The blocks used are incredibly hard-wearing and durable, and come in a variety of patterns. Any pattern could be used to create the design, but the squared surface of the ones chosen here neatly echoes the overall pattern.

As the gravel is loose, it retains its appealing crunchy texture. However, this does mean that it is free to move over the patio if the pockets between the blocks are overfilled, so keep the level below the surface of the blocks.

Plan the positions of the chequerboard details with care, in order to establish the best distribution. As the surface includes loose gravel, it may be best to avoid areas of the patio that are normally under tables and chairs.

1 Prepare the holes by removing paving slabs and adding a layer of hardcore if necessary (see pages 108–9). Use the bolster chisel and hammer to break the stable blocks in half – they should break easily. (Don't worry if the broken edge is uneven as only the surface will be visible.) Arrange the half blocks in the space. When you are happy with the arrangement, lift them one by one and sit them into a bed of wet mortar.

2 Gently tap the blocks into the mortar with the handle of a club hammer and, using a spirit level, check that they are absolutely level with the surface of the surrounding patio.

3 Use a small builder's trowel to pack mortar up around each of the blocks to hold them firm.

4 Fill each pocket with gravel to just below the surface of the blocks. Over time the gravel will settle a little and may need topping up. Keep the level of the gravel below that of the blocks to avoid it moving.

IDEAS TO INSPIRE

• To produce a far mellower finish, use reclaimed red brick and buff gravel in the same way.

• The surface could be softened by planting some of the gravel pockets with small, fragrant creeping thymes. Do this by loosening the layer of hardcore in the base of the pocket and adding a handful of gritty compost. Add a mulch of gravel around the plants.

3

4

Slate spiral patio

Soft blue-green pebbles and green slate combine to produce this cool, tranquil patio.

Encircled by a rendered wall that supports a simple timber bench, the circular patio is just big enough for a small table and chairs. The spiral of slate, uncurling from the centre of the circle, encourages the eye to settle in the space and contributes to the feeling of calm. The strong spiral shape works well in this small area but might be overwhelming in a larger space. When closely packed together, the rounded pebbles form a surprisingly even surface, but visually retain their curves. In stark contrast the slate is angular; its linear form is perfect for reinforcing the direction of the spiral, which really seems to flow around the pebble floor. The two materials are very different in texture, but harmonious in colour, and work together well. The edging of green paddle stones provides a definite, almost pie-crust, edge to the mosaic.

SHOPPING LIST
hardcore
1:4 wet mortar mix (see pages 32–3)
75kg (165lb) of green paddle stones
75kg (165lb) of green slate mulch
250kg (1/4ton) of Japanese green pebbles
1:3 dry mortar mix (see pages 32–3)

TOOLS
stringline and peg
spade
builder's float
trowel
chalk
plank of wood
mallet
rope
brush
watering can with fine rose

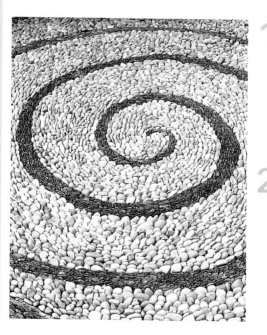

1 Mark out a circle with a radius of 1.5m (5ft) and prepare a firm foundation of hardcore (see pages 28–31). For this particular project it is helpful to have a level base to work on, so apply a thin screed of mortar over the entire circle, using a builder's float to smooth it out.

2 Next, working in small sections, lay a generous bed of mortar at the edge of the circle and push in the paddle stones, set on edge and as close together as possible. As you progress, check the levels (see pages 30–1). If the fall on the edging is correct, then the rest of the patio can be worked from this. Continue until the edge is complete.

3 Mark the centre point of the circle and, using a length of string held at the centre, mark out the inner edge of the border about 30cm (12in) in from the paddlestone edge. Chalk is excellent for marking out on the screed, though not long lasting – sand and spray paint are possible alternatives.

4 Working in sections, lay a ridge of mortar, about 4cm (1½in) wide, on the line and push pieces of slate mulch on edge into the mortar so that the greater part of each piece is in the mortar and the top edge is flat. Pack the pieces as closely together as possible and position them to follow the direction of the curve.

5 Use a spirit level to check that the slate is reasonably level with the edging. If necessary, genty tap the slate further into the mortar using a mallet. Do this very carefully as it is not easy to pull it out.

6 Now start to fill in the border. Spread a layer of mortar about 2.5cm (1in) thick in one section at a time and push in pebbles on their ends so that their tops are just proud of the edge and the slate. Pack the pebbles as closely as you can. The process is time consuming but the more tightly packed the pebbles the more pleasing the finished result will be.

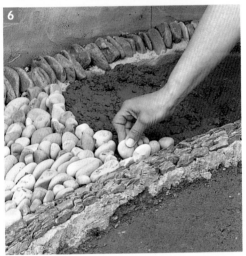

7 When you have completed a 50cm (20in) length of the border, place a board over the surface of the pebbles and gently tap it until the pebbles are forced into the mortar and the board rests on the edging and slate ring. In this way, a level surface is achieved.If the level of the mortar rises too high use less next time. Continue until the border is complete.

8 Next use a length of rope to work out the position of the spiral. Adjust its position until you are happy with its proportions – looking from above is very helpful. Don't be tempted to squeeze in too many circuits. Mark the position of the rope with chalk and remove it.

9 Working from the centre, use the same method employed to build the ring of slate in step 4 to build up the spiral, checking the level against that of the border as you go. Continue until the spiral is complete.

10 Starting from the centre once again, complete the surface by adding pebbles between the lines of the spiral. Remember to cram in as many pebbles as possible and level them with the plank and mallet as before. Allow to set.

11 When the patio is complete, brush the dry mortar mix over the surface. Before starting, check that the pebble surface is completely dry – if it is damp the surface of the pebbles could be stained. The level of the dry mortar should be well below the top of pebbles, so that their character is still apparent. Brush the dry mixture off the surface of the pebbles and very gently sprinkle it with water using a watering can, taking care not to splash it onto the face of the pebbles.

IDEAS TO INSPIRE

• The cool, blue-green of this patio would look superb encircled by a billowing hedge of fragrant lavender 'Hidcote'.

• The spiral design could be executed with any combination of coloured slate and small pebbles to suit your favourite colour theme.

• You could try using a different material for the spiral motif; it could be made up of shards of broken terracotta pot or even a contrasting colour of pebbles.

• For a really subtle finish, the whole surface could be completed with just one type of pebble and the spiral defined only by the direction in which the pebbles are arranged.

Corner patio

Invest one day of hard work and you could be relaxing on this pretty fragrant seating area.

SHOPPING LIST

8cm (3in) deep edging boards
40cm (16in) pegs made from 5cm (2in)
   square timber
preserving woodstain
galvanized nails
3 railway sleepers
weed-suppressing membrane
500kg (½ton) of gravel
creeping plants
large rocks

TOOLS

stringline and peg
tape measure
spade
saw
club hammer
chain saw
spirit level
sharp knife

This informal, all-weather surface is quick and easy to build. It is the perfect place for a bench, or perhaps a table for two, and the ideal solution for brightening up a dingy unused corner. The light-coloured gravel is punctuated by a radiating pattern of chunky railway sleepers. The sleepers are pitted and gnarled, perfect for the informal feel – without them the surface of the gravel would be austere and bland. Fragrant creeping thymes and succulents soften the floor, while large curved, smooth rocks add a little three-dimensional interest. The materials and plants combine to form a harmonious, uncomplicated space with a natural feel.

The quarter circle is probably not large enough for a family patio, but it easily accommodates a bench or small table and chairs, making it the perfect retreat away from the house, for relaxing in the sun or enjoying a good book.

1 Mark out a quarter circle with a radius of 4m (12ft) (see pages 28–9) in your chosen corner and remove any turf and plants from the marked-out area. Keep the curved line of the edge as neat and accurate as possible.

2 Next form the timber edge. Use a hand saw to make cuts in the edging board at 10cm (4in) intervals, cutting only halfway through the wood; if you cut too deeply the board may snap. This makes it flexible enough to bend around the curve neatly. Stain all the timber that needs it.

3 Knock in seven wooden pegs, equally spaced, around the perimeter of the quarter circle, keeping them vertical. These are the pegs to support the edging boards.

4 Hold the edging boards against the outsides of the pegs and bend them gently around the curve; attach them to each peg with nails. Where two lengths of board join, drive in an extra peg and nail both boards to the peg.

5 Cut the railway sleepers in half (this is probably best done with a chain saw, so get help from someone who knows how) and arrange five of the halves as if they are radiating out from the corner, slightly staggering them. Place the most even face of the sleeper uppermost.

6 When you are completely happy with the arrangement, use a spade to mark the position of each of the sleepers and, one by one, remove them and dig a hole to fit the sleeper. The holes should be roughly 10cm (4in) deep, so that 5cm (2in) of the sleeper will be left above the soil.

7 Place the sleeper in the hole, check it is level and firm some of the loose soil back around it to ensure it will not move. Repeat the process with the other sleepers, checking that their surfaces are at the same level as the first.

8 Place a layer of weed-suppressing membrane over the entire area, cutting neatly around the sleepers using a sharp knife and leaving sufficient at the edges to lap up the edging boards. This will prevent weeds from sprouting up through the gravel, making the area easy to maintain.

9 Arrange the plants on top of the membrane in groups, nestling some of them up against the sleepers. Use the sharp knife to cut a cross shape into the membrane to create a planting space for each. Dig a hole and insert the plant.

10 Spread the gravel around the plants and sleepers until it is flush with the surface of the sleepers. Finally, add a few large rocks, bedding them into the surface of the gravel.

IDEAS TO INSPIRE

In a shady corner, grow small, evergreen ferns, such as *Asplenium trichomanes*, tucked into the gravel.

• The design could be extended to complete the circle, creating an unusual round gravel garden, host to a whole range of plants as well as a table and chairs.

• Other low-growing, fragrant plants such as camomile or evergreen grasses could be included in the planting scheme.

Terracotta and pebble patio

Broken terracotta pots are used here to define the pattern in the surface of this earthy pebble mosaic floor.

SHOPPING LIST

hardcore
1:4 wet mortar mix (see pages 32–3)
44 stable or paving blocks
broken terracotta pots
200kg (440lb) of pebbles
1:3 dry mortar mix (see pages 32–3)

TOOLS

stringline and pegs
spade
builder's float
trowel
spirit level
club hammer
plank of wood
mallet
brush
watering can with fine rose

IDEAS TO INSPIRE

• To make an even more conspicuous design, two different-coloured pebbles could be used to complete alternate squares.
• If you have problems collecting enough terracotta, slate mulch could be used to construct the grid.
• Running the lines of the grid at 45 degrees across the space, so that the squares become diamonds, will make the space look wider.

A rigid grid of terracotta shards divides the surface into regular squares and provides a strong colour and textural contrast. The overall effect is quite natural and sits easily amongst the foliage. Surprisingly little terracotta is needed to produce the design, but the contribution of the linear shards is striking. The tightly packed pebbles are very hard-wearing and form a comfortable surface. It would take a while to amass enough broken pots for the project, but garden centres will often give away broken or cracked pots.

1 Mark out and prepare a foundation of hardcore for the patio (see pages 28–31) about 2.3m (7ft 6in) square. It is helpful to have a firm base to work on, so apply a screed of mortar over the compacted hardcore, using a float to spread it out.

2 Using a stringline set up along the edges of the patio as a guide, construct a stable block edge by laying a bed of mortar and pushing the blocks into place. Construct the edge with the correct fall (see pages 30–1); then the rest of the surface can be checked against it.

3 Use the handle of a club hammer to tap the blocks home, and check that they are level with a spirit level.

4 Set up a line to mark the position of the first row of terracotta. Create a mound of mortar along the line about 4cm (1½in) wide and 2.5cm (1in) deep.

5 Push pieces of terracotta into the mortar so that a flat edge is uppermost, a good portion of the shard is embedded in the mortar and the fragment is orientated along the line of mortar. Aim for a band about three shards wide. Keep the surface of the terracotta level with the surface of the edging. Complete all the lines running one way and then those running the other, interlocking them as neatly as possible. Allow the mortar to dry.

6 Fill one of the squares with mortar to just under halfway and make an even layer. Starting at one corner, work systematically across the square, packing in the pebbles set on their ends so that they stand just proud of the terracotta bands. When the square is crammed full, place a plank over the square and tap it down until the pebble surface is flush with that of the terracotta. Repeat until all of the squares are complete.

7 Brush the dry mix over the surface of the pebbles and terracotta. Leave enough depth of pebbles exposed to retain their individual character. Brush all of the dry mix off the surface of the pebbles or it may stain. Use a watering can with a fine rose to wet the dry mix.

Templates

Select the relevant template and copy and enlarge it
to the size you need for your project.

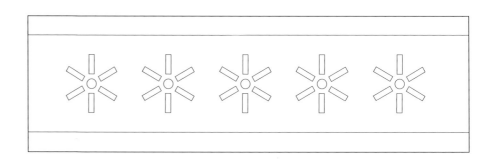

Daisy Trough plus alternative designs,

see pages 44–7

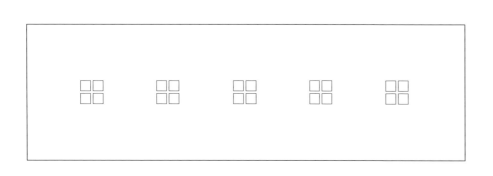

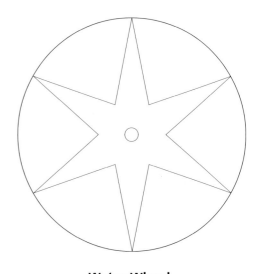

Water Wheel,

see pages 56–9

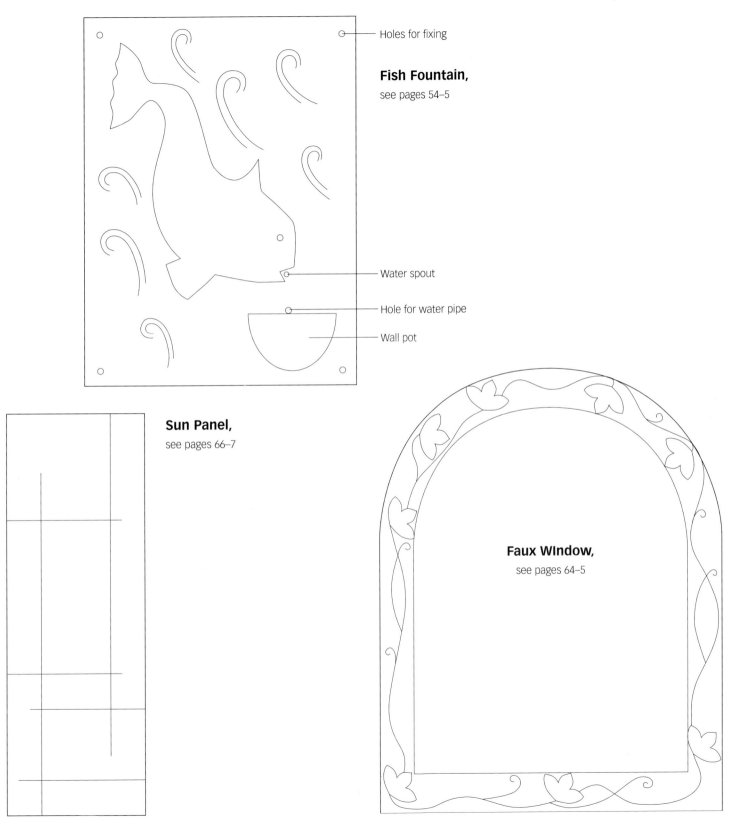

Holes for fixing

Fish Fountain,
see pages 54–5

Water spout

Hole for water pipe

Wall pot

Sun Panel,
see pages 66–7

Faux Window,
see pages 64–5

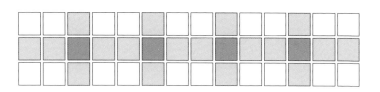

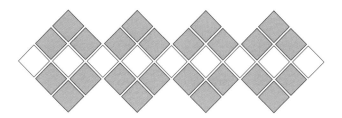

Moorish frieze plus alternative designs,

see pages 68–71

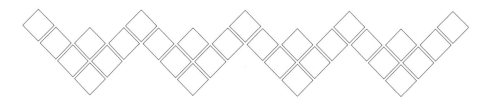

Citrus Dining Table,

see pages 76–9

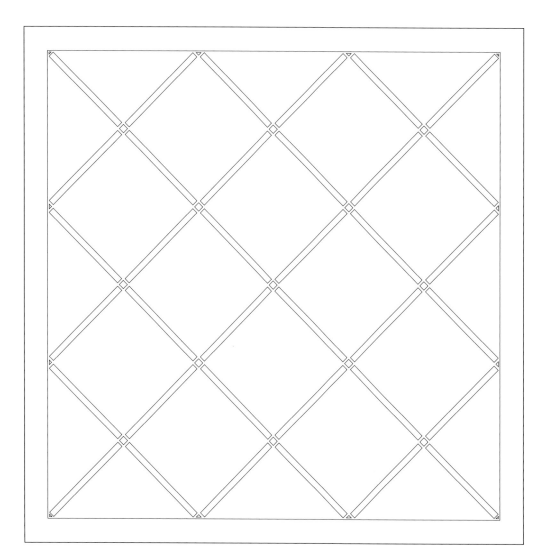

Butler's Tray Table,
see pages 82–3

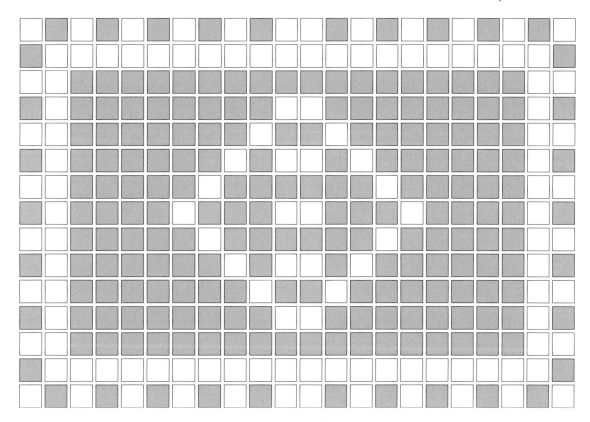

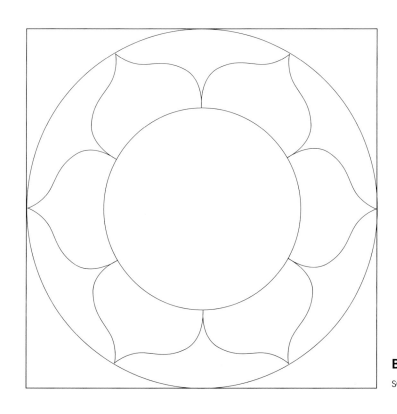

Beaded Centrepiece,
see pages 102-5

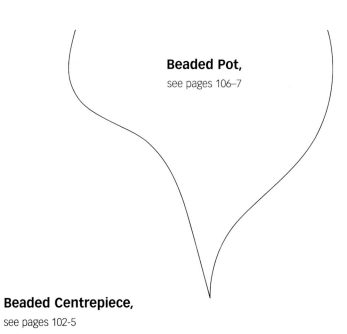

Beaded Pot,
see pages 106–7

Acknowledgements

Author's Acknowledgements

My thanks:

To Mark Bolton for his stunning photography, his willingness to 'muck-in' and his unfailing sense of humour.

To the team at Hamlyn for all their support and enthusiasm for the project, especially Sarah Ford, Abi Rowsell and Geoff Fennell.

To Joanna smith for her copy editing expertise.

To my parents, Ruth and Geoffrey Smee, for all their encouragement, tireless practical assistance in ways too numerous to mention and once again surrendering part of their garden to my projects.

To my brother, Grahame Smee for his unstinting support.

To the staff of Grovelands Garden Centre, Shinfield, especially Darren Corbett, for all their help.

To Steve Lechavalier of Specialist Aggregates for sourcing the perfect pebbles and glass.

To the staff of Gardenscape Supplies, Playhatch, for all their assistance.

And to David as always for everything.

Picture Acknowledgements in Source Order

Corbis/ © Patrick Ward 74 top

John Glover 10 bottom left, 100, 101, /Designer: Karen Maskell/ RHS Hampton Court Flower Show 1999 21 right, /RHS Chelsea Flower Show 1993 36, /Designer: Peter Styles/ RHS Chelsea Flower Show 1996 15 top left.

Octopus Publishing Group Limited/Mark Bolton front cover, back cover, Front flap, back flap, 1, 3 left, 4, 5, 6 bottom, 7 bottom right, 19 right, 21 left, 22, 23, 24, 25, 26, 27, 28 right, 28 centre, 29, 30, 31 centre left, 32, 33, 34-35, 35, 38, 39, 40, 41, 42-43, 44, 45, 46, 47, 48-49, 50-51, 51, 55, 56, 57, 58-59, 60-61, 64, 65, 66-67, 68-69, 70-71, 72-73, 76-77, 78-79, 80-81, 82-83, 84-85, 85, 89 right, 90, 90 left, 91 top, 91 bottom, 92 bottom, 93 top, 93 bottom, 94 left, 94 bottom right, 95, 96, 97 left, 97 right, 98-99, 99 right, 102 left, 102 right, 103, 104, 105 Top, 105 bottom, 106, 107 left, 107 right, 108, 109 left, 109 right, 110, 111 left, 111 right, 112 left, 112 right, 113, 114, 114-115, 116 left, 116 right, 117, 118 top, 118-119 bottom, 119 right, 119 top left, 120, 121, 121 top, /Mark Bolton / Designer: Ellie Hawkins 87 left, /Tom Mannion 7 bottom left, 37 left, /Stephen Robson 9, 15 bottom centre, /Mel Yates 18-19, /Mark Bolton / Hannah Genders Garden Design / RHS Chelsea Flower Show 2002 86 left, /Mark Bolton/ Bracknell & District Gardening Club/ RHS Chelsea Flower Show 2001 31 bottom left, /Mark Bolton/ Designer Mrs B. Lay/ RHS Hampton Court Flower Show 2001 3 right, /Mark Bolton/ Designer: Geoffrey Whiten/ RHS Chelsea Flower Show 2001 31 right, /Mark Bolton/ Designer: Michael Miller & the Prince's Foundation Vita Dept/ RHS Chelsea Flower Show 2001 20 left, /Mark Bolton/ Elizabeth Apedaile Design & Dove Landscapes/ RHS Hampton Court Flower Show 2001 14 top, /Mark Bolton/ Pots n Plants of Masham/ RHS Hampton Court Flower Show 2001 17 bottom right, David Sarton/ Designer: City & Guilds Gardening Design Class/ RHS Hampton Court Flower Show 2002 20 right, /David Sarton/ Designer: Maya Drummond/ RHS Hampton Court Flower Show 2002 7 top.

Jerry Harpur 52 top, 74 bottom, /Chaumont Festival 1999 16 bottom right, /Designer: Bob Clark, Berkeley, California, USA 11 bottom left, /Designer: Topher Delaney/ San Diego Children's hospital, USA 52 bottom, /Designer:Topher Delaney/ San Diego Children's Hospital, USA 11 centre right, /Designer: Margot Knox , Melbourne, Australia 10 centre left, /Designer: Margot Knox, Melbourne, Australia 75, /Takako Scott 11 bottom right, /Designer: Phillip Watson, USA 37 right, /Bill Willis, Marrakech 12-13.

Andrew Lawson/ Designer: James Aldridge 10 right, /RHS Chelsea Flower Show 2001 8-9, 11 top right, /Designer: Margot Knox, Melbourne, Australia 63, /The Old Rectory, Sudborough, UK 28 left, /RHS Rosemoor, Devon 86 right.

Marianne Majerus/ Designer: Ann Frith 6 top, /Designer: Bunny Guinness 17 bottom left, /Museo Sorolla, Madrid 62, /Designer: Michele Osborne 15 top right, /RHS Hampton Court 2000 16 bottom centre, /Designer: Judy Wiseman 15 bottom left.

Clive Nichols/Sue Berger 11 top left, /Blakedown Landscapes/ RHS Chelsea Flower Show 1998 14 bottom, /Designer: Belinda Eade/ 'Gardens Illustrated' Garden/ RHS Chelsea Flower Show 1994 53, /Designer: Ann Frith (pond) / Simon Arnold (mirror) 17 top, /Andrew & Karla Newell 15 bottom right.